MW00679838

a Different Angle
Co-operActivities in Communication

a Different Angle
Co-operActivities in Communication

By MICHELLE BUEHRING

JOAN ASHKENAS, Editor

Illustrations by
SUSAN ENGELMAN BLOCK

JAG PUBLICATIONS

© 1998 JAG Publications

Co-operActivities is a registered trademark of JAG Publications.

All Rights Reserved. No part of the publication may be reproduced or transmitted in any form or by any means without the written permission of the publisher.

Published by:
JAG Publications
11288 Ventura Boulevard
Studio City, California 91604
Telephone and Fax: 818 505-9002
email address: info@jagpublications-esl.com

Design and Production by Jack Lanning

Printed in the United States of America

10 9 8 7 6 5 4 3 2

Library of Congress catalog card number 98-65319

ISBN 0-943327-19-9

Contents

To the Students...   *vii*

Talking With *A Different Angle*   *1*

CHAPTER 1   **If the Shoe Were on the Other Foot...?** *A case of animal cruelty*   *2*
Co-operActivities: **Comparing Notes**
     Character Role-play
     Vocabulary Mini-bingo

CHAPTER 2   **A Test of Honesty** *Standing up for your rights*   *6*
Co-operActivities: **Role-play Rotation**
     The $25,000 Vocabulary Game

CHAPTER 3   **Up in Smoke** *Marijuana and the law*   *12*
Co-operActivities: **Half the Story**
     Timed Reactions
     Sharing Adjectives
     Paragraph Skit

CHAPTER 4   **On Guard** *Rights for the disabled*   *17*
Co-operActivities: **Making Predictions from the Beginning**
     Pair Reading by Paragraphs
     Reconstruct the Story

CHAPTER 5   **Really, Really Getting Rid of Smallpox** *Keeping viruses alive*   *21*
Co-operActivities: **Back to Back Dictation**
     Finish the Story
     Situation Role-play

CHAPTER 6   **A Pilot's Bill of Rights** *Age discrimination*   *30*
Co-operActivities: **Send the Messenger!**
     A Personal Web Page
     Interview a Classmate

CHAPTER 7   **Troubled Waters** *An environmental question*   *35*
Co-operActivities: **Making Predictions from the End**
     Story Relay Race
     The Most For; The Most Against
     Vocabulary Through Pictures
     Giving Directions

CHAPTER 8   **A Long, Long Time Ago...** *Crime and politics*   *41*
Co-operActivities: **Guess the Facts**
     Building a Word Domain
     The Debate
     Bingo

CHAPTER 9 **Got a Cigarette?** *Misguiding the public* 48
Co-operActivities: **Introduction Cloze**
Question Exchange
Role-play Interview

CHAPTER 10 **Is Shakespeare Really Dead?** *The liberal vs. the conservative* 54
Co-operActivities: **Pair Dictation**
Pros Meet Cons
Memory Cloze
The 45-Second Board Game

CHAPTER 11 **Whose Child Is He, Anyway?** *A case of children's rights* 61
Co-operActivities: **Half the Summary**
A Detailed Image

CHAPTER 12 **Do You Believe...?** *The UFO cover-up* 66
Co-operActivities: **Share a Picture**
Sentence-completion Guess
Reading Role-play
True or False Stories

CHAPTER 13 **To Treat or Not to Treat** *AIDS and ethics* 72
Co-operActivities: **The Missing Words**
Paragraph Outline
Facts and Opinions Exchange

CHAPTER 14 **Standing Tall** *Defending your beliefs* 77
Co-operActivities: **Comparing Guesses**
You're Hot / You're Cold
Retell the Story
Word Associations
Classroom Feud
Dialog Role-play

CHAPTER 15 **Given Half a Chance** *Gun control in America* 82
Co-operActivities: **Timed Reading**
The Police Line-up
The Trial

Survey Pages 95

Sources 102

To the Students...

As English language learners, joining in a conversation is sometimes not an easy thing to do. Many students feel they need certain information or feel they don't have enough vocabulary to talk intelligently about a topic. Others don't have confidence in expressing their own opinions on a subject. The goal of *A Different Angle* is to give you the opportunity to discuss some very important and controversial issues affecting American society today. *A Different Angle* also helps you to understand the similarities and differences of values across cultures.

The stories in the textbook are extremely interesting and really make you think. The activities and exercises help you understand the subject matter and reinforce new vocabulary. They are lively and fun to do. You get a lot of opportunity to speak up and give your opinions on the different topics in the book. You don't have to be afraid to say what you think because there are no right or wrong answers.

A Different Angle wants you to be successful in your daily life as well as in the classroom. The author also wishes you many exciting conversations in the future.

Talking with *A Different Angle*

An opinion is a statement which reflects a personal, individual feeling.
Everyone has an opinion. Try using these expressions for your discussions.

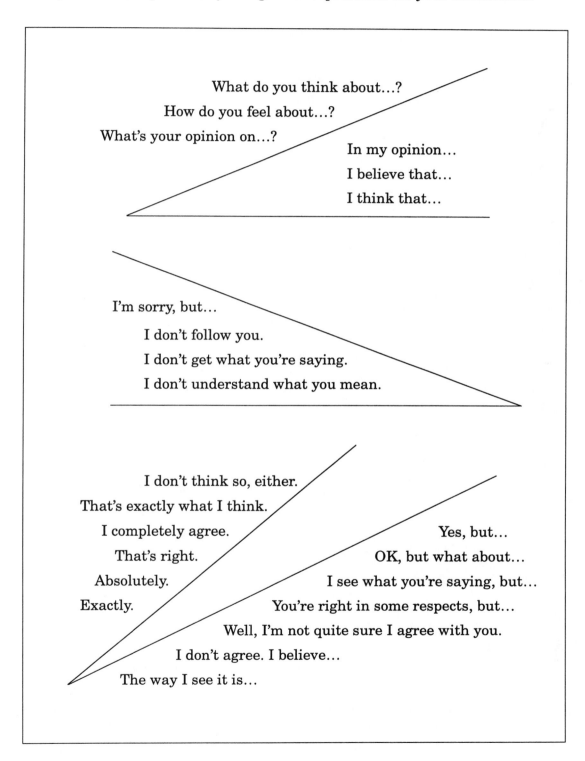

What do you think about...?
How do you feel about...?
What's your opinion on...?

In my opinion...
I believe that...
I think that...

I'm sorry, but...
I don't follow you.
I don't get what you're saying.
I don't understand what you mean.

I don't think so, either.
That's exactly what I think.
I completely agree.
That's right.
Absolutely.
Exactly.

Yes, but...
OK, but what about...
I see what you're saying, but...
You're right in some respects, but...
Well, I'm not quite sure I agree with you.
I don't agree. I believe...
The way I see it is...

CHAPTER 1

If the Shoe Were on the Other Foot...?

WARM-UP

In pairs or in a group, discuss the answers to these questions.

1. How are animals and humans alike? How are they different?
2. What kind of relationship do you think people ought to have with their pets?
3. Talk about one experience (good or bad) that you had with an animal.
4. Do you think animals should be used in medical research?

Co-operActivity

COMPARING NOTES

Take notes as your teacher tells you the story. Compare your notes with your group so you can fill in any missing information. Ask your teacher questions to help you complete your understanding of the story.

If the Shoe Were on the Other Foot...?

A case of animal cruelty

LOS ANGELES, August 8, 1995 — "Was he or was he not cruel to the animal?" That is what a jury must decide about Alan Roberts, the man who beat a dog to death with a baseball bat for attacking his 19-month-old son. Now Alan Roberts, 29, of Huntington Beach, might have to pay a $20,000 fine and spend as much as one year in jail. Here's what happened:

On July 30, Roberts stopped at a coffee shop while his wife and son, Andrew, waited outside. According to witnesses, an 8-month old Akita dog ran from its owner's house. Suddenly, it approached and attacked the child, biting him and clamping down on his face, forehead and nose. The mother was finally able to separate the dog from the boy.

The boy "was covered with blood" Roberts told reporters. "I held him to my chest and took him to the hospital." Andrew received about 60 stitches, mostly on his face, at Huntington Beach Medical Center.

An hour after the attack, Roberts drove back to the neighborhood with a baseball bat to look for the dog. He found it tied to a fence outside of April Wyld's apartment. According to police reports, Roberts brutally clubbed the dog 15 times while it was tied to the fence. The dog later died at a veterinary hospital.

The dog's owner, April Wyld, 28, of Huntington Beach called the Orange County People For Animals, a private animal activist organization in Irvine. They encouraged her to make a criminal case against Roberts.

According to the law, it is a misdemeanor crime to hurt an animal intentionally. Roberts, a 29-year-old roofer, told reporters that all he thought about was his child's pain and that his son could possibly die. "Up until that point my life has been pretty quiet. I was very confused." he added.

"The dog was my life; he was so special," Wyld said when reporters interviewed her. The dog had never bitten anyone before.

HELPFUL VOCABULARY

attack – to use violence to hurt someone

charge – an official statement saying that someone is guilty of a crime

witness – someone who sees an accident or a crime and can describe what happened

clamp – hold something tightly so that it doesn't move

brutal – very cruel and violent

veterinary hospital – animal hospital

activist – someone who works for social or political change

encourage – to help someone become brave or confident enough to do something

misdemeanor – a crime that is not very serious

RAPID REPLY

Write answers to these questions immediately.

1. The story took place in what city? _____

2. The dog attack occurred
    a. in front of the dog owner's home
    b. in a parking lot
    c. at a baseball field

3. (**T-F**) The mother was able to separate the dog from her child but not without some help.

4. Andrew, the boy, received _____ stitches, mostly on his face.

5. Where did the dog actually die? _____

6. What was the name of the organization that supported April Wyld, the dog's owner? _____

7. What did the organization encourage April to do?

    _____

8. If Roberts is found guilty of this crime, how much time could he spend in jail? _____

A CLOSER LOOK

1. Look at the title of the story. What do you think it means?

    _____

2. List the three most important details of the story here.
    a.
    b.
    c.

    Do you and your classmates agree?

3. Imagine that you are the reporter who wrote this newspaper article. Write a headline that you think would attract readers to your story.

    _____

CLASS EXERCISES

- In small groups, discuss the question:

    Should the man go to jail for killing the dog?

As you discuss the question, consider the reasons before making a personal decision. Refer to the story at any time during the discussion. It is not necessary to make a group decision. Use the workspace on the next page for your ideas.

Why Roberts should go to jail.

1.

2.

3.

4.

5.

Why Roberts should not go to jail.

1.

2.

3.

4.

5.

Additional Comments:

Your personal decision:

Co-operActivity

CHARACTER ROLE-PLAY

Create small groups. Each person in a group takes the part of one of the characters, e.g., the father, the mother, the dog owner, the child, the dog. Discuss your feelings.

Co-operActivity

VOCABULARY MINI-BINGO

Select 4 words from the "Helpful Vocabulary" list. Write one word in each box. Listen to the word definitions your teacher reads, and mark off each word as soon as you hear its definition. The first student to mark off all 4 words is the winner!

CHAPTER 2

A Test of Honesty

BRIAN DALTON

WARM-UP

In pairs or in a group, discuss the answers to these questions.

1. How do you feel before you take a test?
2. Do you think it is necessary for students to take tests?
3. How much importance should be given to test scores when deciding a student's grade in a course?
4. Tell your partner or group about a memorable test experience you had (good or bad).

- Look at the picture of Brian Dalton. What kind of person do you think Brian is? What do you think the story is about?

You and a partner will be assigned a section of the story. With your partner, review your section's contents and vocabulary, so that you can explain it to others.

A TEST OF HONESTY

Standing up for your rights

QUEENS, New York, May, 1992—High school senior Brian Dalton left the Scholastic Aptitude Test (SAT) testing room in Queens, NY feeling certain that he did well on the college entrance exam. All he needed was a score of 700 or better for an athletic scholarship at St. John's University, the nearby college that his 20-year-old brother attends. In fact, Brian did so well on his SATs that the Educational Testing Service (ETS) thinks he cheated. Here's what happened.

Brian Dalton is a senior at Holy Cross High School in Queens. When he first took the SAT in May 1991, he scored a total of 620 points out of a possible 1600. Dissatisfied with his performance, he registered and took another SAT test six months later (in November) and received a score of 1030, a 410-point increase.

The ETS immediately became suspicious. "The chances of a student increasing his score by that amount are rare," ETS president told reporters. He added, "We must question high score increases to protect the honor of the test. For example, we would question scores that go up 350 points. Yet Dalton's score increased by 410 points!"

Actually, Brian had no idea that there was any problem with his test scores until he called the ETS two weeks after he had taken the November test to see if he could get his scores sent home early. As a star swimmer at Holy Cross High School, Brian was hoping to get a scholarship to St. John's University and wanted to start applying for it. The ETS told him that they could not release his scores because they suspected that someone had taken the test for him. "I couldn't believe they thought I cheated!" Brian told reporters.

When Brian was a sophomore in high school, he took the PSAT (a practice SAT) as did many in his class. His score on that test was very similar to his score on the SAT he took in May, but not to his November SAT taken just six months later. Besides that, the ETS told Brian that his signatures on the May and November tests didn't match.

The ETS offered Brian two choices: go to court to fight or retake the test. The testing center recently won a court case in which a student admitted he took an exam for another student.

Brian says he did not cheat on the test. So, he and his parents decided to sue the ETS to have his November test score approved and asked for more than $300,000. Brian has had to delay applying to colleges until the lawsuit has been decided. He may have also lost his chance for a swimming scholarship.

Brian is a C-plus student and agrees that he doesn't usually test well. He says that he didn't take the PSAT seriously because he thought it was just a practice test. He also says his May test scores were low because he had mononucleosis when he took the exam.

Brian says that his scores may have increased so much because he attended a six-week SAT prep course from Princeton Review. (Princeton Review gives one of the nation's largest SAT preparation courses.) "I really learned a lot," said Brian. Not surprisingly, the Princeton Review company supports Brian, and with all the free publicity of the case, has agreed to pay for half of Brian's legal expenses. However, John Katzman, president of Princeton Review, did admit to reporters that 150 points is an average gain for students who take the prep course.

Peter Dalton, Brian's father and a New York City police detective, and Joann Dalton, Brian's mother and a secretary for the New York City Board of Education, are furious with the ETS. Starting his own investigation, Peter Dalton contacted a test administrator who said he saw Brian at the test. He also found two students who said they saw Brian there. In addition, Peter Dalton gave Brian's signature to a second analyst who said it matched other samples of his signature. Peter was also ready to have Brian's score sheet fingerprinted, but the ETS refused.

At one point when Brian realized the stress this situation was causing his family, he decided to retake the test. His parents, however, convinced him not to.

HELPFUL VOCABULARY

The **SAT** (Scholastic Aptitude Test), is managed by the ETS, a national testing service in Princeton, New Jersey that also gives the TOEFL (Test of English as a Foreign Language) and other tests such as the GRE (The Graduate Record Exam) and the NTE (The National Teacher's Exam).

athletic – able to play a sport (or sports) very well

scholarship – an amount of money given to someone by an organization to help pay for his or her education

dissatisfied – unhappy

suspect – think that someone may be dishonest or guilty of a crime

sue – make a legal claim against someone, especially for money, because s/he has harmed you in some way

lawsuit – a problem or complaint that someone brings to the court to be settled, especially for money

mononucleosis – an infectious illness that makes you feel weak and tired for a long time

prep course – preparation course

gain – increase

detective – police officer whose job it is to solve mysteries

furious – very angry

investigation – an attempt to find out the reasons for something, such as a crime or scientific problem

RAPID REPLY

Write answers to these questions immediately.

1. Where does this story take place?

   _____

2. What score did Brian need? _____

   _____

3. What organization was Brian fighting against? _____

4. What score did Brian receive on his first SAT exam? _____

5. What was his score on the exam six months later? _____

6. Brian decided to call the testing center for his SAT results because

   a. he was too excited to wait for the results to come in the mail.

   b. the results were never delivered to him but were sent directly to the college of his choice.

   c. he needed to apply for a scholarship.

7. What two things about Brian's second SAT exam alarmed the testing center?

   a.

   b.

8. (**T-F**) Brian was a C+ student.

9. What were the reasons Brian gave for not performing well on the PSAT?

_____

10. According to the story, Brian wanted to retake the test but
   a. his parents told him not to.
   b. his lawyer told him not to.
   c. the ETS said he couldn't.

A CLOSER LOOK

1. Look at the title of the story. What do you think it means?

_____

2. List the four most important details of the story here.
   a.

   b.

   c.

   d.

   Do you and your classmates agree?

3. Imagine that you are the reporter who wrote this newspaper article. Write a headline that you think would attract readers to your story.

_____

4. **Sequence Jumble**

   Order the sentences according to how the events happened in the story. Number 1 has been done for you.

   _____ Brian called the ETS to get his scores.

   _____ Brian received a score of 620 on his SAT exam.

   _____ Brian's test scores alarmed the ETS.

   _____ Brian took the ETS to court.

   _____ Brian took the SAT again in November 1991.

   _____ Brian's father decided to do his own investigation.

   _____ Brian took a prep course.

   _____ The ETS would not give Brian his scores.

   __1__ Brian took the SAT in May.

   _____ The ETS told Brian they thought he cheated on the exam.

   _____ Brian was about to apply for a scholarship to St. John's.

   _____ Brian could not believe the ETS thought he cheated.

   _____ Brian received a score of 1030 on his SAT exam.

CLASS EXERCISES

- In small groups, support your opinions about the questions below.

  Do you think Brian took the test?

  Do you think he should retake the test?

  Use the workspace that follows to write down any notes from your discussion you may want to recall.

  _____

  _____

  _____

  _____

  _____

  _____

  _____

  _____

  _____

Co-operActivity

ROLE-PLAY ROTATION

Choose a character in the story. (Be creative! There are many.) Next, the class forms a double line, so each student, i.e. each character, is face to face with another character. You have two minutes to tell each other your opinion of what happened in the story and what the outcome should be. Stay in a double line formation, and just rotate to the next character every two minutes until you have spoken to all the characters in the story.

Co-operActivity

THE $25,000 VOCABULARY GAME

The class is divided into two teams. Each team should choose a team name. You and another member of your team form pairs, and each pair sits face to face, so that one of you can see the board and the other can't.

The teacher will write five vocabulary words from the story on the board. The student who can see the words tries to get his or her partner to say each word by giving explanations and examples orally, as well as using gestures and/or pictures. For example, if one of the words is "cat," the clue-giver might say to his partner, "This is a small furry animal. People usually have this animal as a pet." The clue-giver may also decide to quickly draw a picture of a cat on a piece of paper. Of course, the clue giver can never use the word or any part of it in his or her explanation.

When you and your partner have finished all five words, you can help your teammates. The team to finish all five words first, gets a point. For the next round, switch places with your partner, and your teacher begins again with five different words on the board. The first team to get five points is the winner.

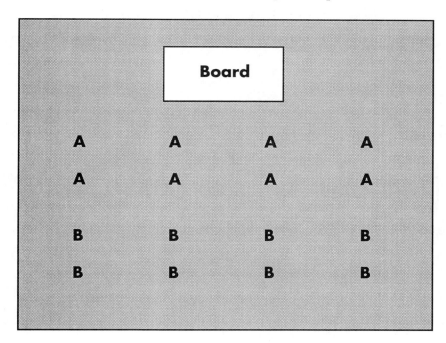

CHAPTER 3

Up in Smoke

WARM-UP

With a partner — talk about a teacher you loved.
— talk about a teacher you hated.
— discuss what you think the qualities of an ideal teacher are.
" An ideal teacher should have/be…"

(rank the qualities in order of importance)

Co-operActivity

HALF THE STORY

Take notes as you listen to your teacher tell you one half of the story. Consult with the members of your group to be sure you understand the vocabulary, the content and any specific details. When you are ready, you will meet with a partner who has the other half of the story. Explain your half to your partner, so that he or she understands it as well as you do. When you hear your partner's half of the story, be sure to ask any questions that will help you to understand that portion clearly.

UP IN SMOKE

Marijuana and the law

CHICAGO, Illinois, December 1995—Michael Maynard was a dedicated, hard-working teacher. He had been employed at Bloom Township High School, outside of Chicago, for almost two years. He had a natural ability to understand teenagers and a reputation among the faculty for motivating his students. He loved his job, and his students loved him. Then, on the eve of winter break in December 1995, he was fired. Here's why.

Michael Maynard had been arrested in 1974 for possession of less than half an ounce (10 grams) of marijuana.

In 1974, Michael was a 20-year-old college student, and like many young students of the time, says he occasionally smoked "pot." He had been involved in a minor traffic accident, and when the police searched his car they found a small plastic bag of marijuana. He said he was guilty and paid a fine of $100. That was all. In fact, the situation seemed so minor that Michael forgot that it ever happened.

In 1979, the State of Illinois passed a law designed to protect schoolchildren from convicted criminals. The law was expanded in 1985 to require that schools check the backgrounds of its teachers as well. The law says that schools must fire any teacher who has committed a crime including minor drug offenses. A standard background check on Michael revealed his marijuana offense, and the school board immediately told him he had to go.

Michael was stunned at his sudden termination. He had just begun his teaching career at the encouragement of his wife and children. Before becoming a teacher, Michael had tried a career in politics and, after that, in business but was unsuccessful in both.

Even though Michael is not allowed to appeal the decision (the law does not permit appeals), he has chosen to fight back. With the help of a lawyer, he is trying to have the 1985 Illinois law rewritten so that it includes a review board that decides who can or can't teach. He told reporters, "I didn't even know the incident was on my record!" And with the same kind of passion he uses when he teaches he declared, "I'm a good teacher!"

HELPFUL VOCABULARY

dedicated – serious about one's work
reputation – the opinion people have of someone or something
possession – the state of having or owning something
pot – (slang) marijuana
minor – small, not very important or serious
convicted – proved guilty of a crime
expanded – widened
commit a crime – do something wrong or illegal
reveal – show something previously hidden
offense – crime
standard – usual or normal
stunned – shocked, extremely surprised
termination – end; firing from a job
encourage – help someone become confident or brave enough to do something
appeal – request a higher court to reconsider the decision of a lower court
incident – event

RAPID REPLY

Write answers to these questions immediately.

1. At what school did Michael teach? _____

2. Michael was well-liked by students and faculty because

   _____

3. Why was Michael arrested? _____

4. Why had he been stopped by police? _____

5. (**T-F**) Michael had forgotten about his arrest because
   a.   the drugs destroyed his memory of that night.
   b.   he thought it was "no big deal."
   c.   it was such a long time ago.

6. The 1979 law passed by the State of Illinois dealt with
   a.   finding drugs.
   b.   protecting children.
   c.   encouraging education.

7. Which career did Michael have before becoming a teacher?

   _____

8. How does Michael want to change the 1985 state law?

   _____

9. In which city did this story take place? _____

A CLOSER LOOK

1. Look at the title of the story. What do you think it means?

   _____

2. List the four most important details of the story here.
   a.
   b.
   c.
   d.

Do you and your classmates agree?

3. Below are 5 individual statements. Some are facts; some are opinions. Label each statement using **F** for **FACT** and **O** for **OPINION** in the space provided.

_____ a. Michael Maynard was a dedicated and caring teacher.

_____ b. He had been working at the high school for almost two years.

_____ c. The police searched Michael's car and found marijuana.

_____ d. Michael was stunned at his sudden termination.

_____ e. Michael wants the law that got him fired to be rewritten.

CLASS EXERCISES
Co-operActivity

TIMED REACTIONS

Consider the questions below carefully. Quickly write down any ideas you have about them. You will have a time limit in which to give your opinion for each of the questions to your group. You may react to any statement made by another member of your group during your time limit.

> — Should Michael Maynard be allowed to teach?
> — Do you think he'll win his case?
> — Do you think marijuana is a dangerous drug?
> — Do you think marijuana should be legalized?
> — Studies have shown that there are chemicals in marijuana that lessen the intense pain of patients suffering from arthritis, cancer, AIDS or the effects of chemotherapy treatment. Should marijuana be used for medical purposes?
> — Are drugs a big problem in your country?

• In the previous timed-exercise:

Which questions were easy to talk about with your group?

Which questions were difficult to talk about with your group?

Which questions do you wish you had more time to talk about?

Co-operActivity

SHARING ADJECTIVES

A teacher is not only the person who stands in front of a classroom. A teacher can be anyone who "gives a lesson" or shows you how to do something. Think of a person in your life from whom you have learned an important lesson (a relative, a world figure etc.). Draw a picture of him/her on a piece of paper. To go along with your drawing, choose 5 descriptive adjectives that represent this person's character and write them below the picture. Share your drawings and adjectives with your classmates. Check with your teacher for some fun activities to do with your drawings.

Co-operActivity

PARAGRAPH SKIT

Each group in the class chooses a paragraph and writes it in play form. Have fun acting out your portion of the story, and enjoy watching your classmates, too!

SURVEY

Survey at least 3 people to get more information and opinions about drugs in American society.

AGREE or DISAGREE?	Comments
1. The legal drinking age for alcohol should be lowered to 18 years old.	
2. Drunk driving laws are too severe.	
3. Marijuana should be legalized.	
4. Cigarette smoking should not be permitted in restaurants.	
5. The jail time for selling marijuana should be equal to the jail time for selling heroin.	
6. Having a daily glass of wine means you're an alcoholic.	
7. Tobacco and alcohol are not drugs.	
8. There should be periodic drug testing done in the workplace.	
9. Drug dealers can receive the death penalty if a death results from their drug sale.	

CHAPTER 4
On Guard

WARM-UP *Co-operActivity: MAKING PREDICTIONS FROM THE BEGINNING*

- Below are the first two paragraphs of the story. Read the paragraphs and, with your partner or group, make predictions about the problem in the story. Afterwards, share your ideas with the whole class.

NEWTON, Mass., April, 1995—The new rules used by the national YMCA have changed the career of lifeguard director, David Schultz. Here's what happened.

David Schultz was told last summer that he could no longer be a lifeguard at the YMCA swimming pool in North Attleboro. Even though he had a perfect record of nearly two years, David's YMCA lifeguard certification was taken away from him. He was given a job as a program assistant which paid him $8,000 less.

Co-operActivity

READING BY PARAGRAPHS

You will be asked to read the story "On Guard" paragraph by paragraph. In other words, you will read one paragraph silently and then stop. You and a partner will have a few minutes to help each other understand the paragraph. When you have finished, read the next paragraph silently and stop again, so you and your partner can confirm each other's understanding of that paragraph. Follow the same procedure until you have read the whole story.

ON GUARD

Rights for the disabled

NEWTON, Mass., April, 1995—The new rules used by the national YMCA have changed the career of lifeguard director, David Schultz. Here's what happened.

David Schultz was told last summer that he could no longer be a lifeguard at the YMCA swimming pool in North Attleboro. Even though he had a perfect record of nearly two years, David's YMCA lifeguard certification was taken away from him. He was given a job as a pro-gram assistant which paid him $8,000 less.

David is deaf. According to the new policies brought to the YMCA in 1994, lifeguards must be able to "hear noises and danger signals."

Gerald DeMers, a physical-education professor who helped write the Y's swimming regulations explained to reporters, "You are using all your senses all of the time when you're guarding the water. If you're looking in one direction and don't hear a swimmer yelling for help, he can very quickly slip below the surface of the water."

Ella Mae Hope disagrees. David taught her two children to swim at the YMCA in Massachusetts. She says that careful atten-tion is what really matters for a lifeguard. In support of David she told reporters, "I've seen lifeguards talking to pretty girls at the beach and not even paying attention to the water."

David argues that he is especially alert because of his deafness. He is proud of his past record of over 20 rescues since 1979.

Last December David sued the YMCA USA for $20 million. He says he is not being judged fairly and he wants his old job back. He is charging that the "Y" is discriminating against him by ignoring his past safety record. David's lawyer says that the YMCA's action is in direct violation of the 1990 Americans With Disabilities Act.

HELPFUL VOCABULARY

career – job that someone is trained for

certification – an official paper that states something is true

policy – an organization's rules for doing something

senses – abilities; sight, hearing, touch, taste, smell

alert – always watching and ready to notice anything unusual or dangerous

rescue – save someone from harm or danger

sue – make a legal claim against someone, especially for money, because s/he has harmed you in some way

judge – form or give an opinion about someone or something after thinking about all the information

charge – say officially that someone is guilty of a crime

disability – a physical or mental condition that makes it difficult for someone to do the things that most people are able to do.

ignore – not pay attention to someone or something

violation – against the law

RAPID REPLY

Write answers to these questions immediately.

1. What is the name of the organization that David Schultz works for?

   _____

2. What happened to David's job?

   _____

3. What did the new YMCA policy say?

   _____

4. What was the argument Ella Mae Hope gave in support of David?

   _____

5. How many people has David saved during his career as a lifeguard?

   _____

6. What argument is David using to claim discrimination?

   _____

   _____

A CLOSER LOOK

1. List the four most important details of "On Guard" here.
   a.
   b.
   c.
   d.

   Do you and your classmates agree?

Co-operActivity

RECONSTRUCT THE STORY

Reconstruct David's story using the following key words. Work with a partner(s).

rules   YMCA   David Schultz   lifeguard   lower paying job
senses   pretty girls   rescues   sue   disability

CLASS EXERCISES

- In pairs or in a group, discuss these questions.

1. How are the disabled treated in your country?

2. What differences and/or similarities do you see in the way the disabled are treated in this country compared to your country?

3. Do you personally know anyone who is disabled? What is his or her life like?

4. Do you think swimmers are less safe with David as lifeguard than with a lifeguard who can hear.

5. How would you feel if *your* children were swimming in the pool with David as the lifeguard?

6. Do you think he will win the lawsuit?

POEM TRANSLATION

Translate each sentence of the following poem into your native language.

A BAG OF TOOLS   _____

Isn't it strange   _____

That princes and kings,   _____

And clowns that caper   _____

In sawdust rings,   _____

And common people   _____

Like you and me   _____

Are builders for eternity?   _____

Each is given a bag of tools, _____

A shapeless mass,   _____

A book of rules;   _____

And each must make–   _____

Ere life is flown–   _____

A stumbling block   _____

Or a stepping stone.   _____

        R. L. Sharpe (1890)

Write your reaction to the poem here.

_____

_____

_____

_____

_____

_____

CHAPTER 5

Really, Really Getting Rid of Smallpox

WARM-UP *Co-operActivity: BACK TO BACK DICTATION*

You are sitting back to back with a partner. You are either **Student A**, pages 22 and 23 or **Student B**, pages 24 and 25. Find and look only at your dictation page. You and your partner will dictate the information you have to each other **only once** until you have completed the entire passage. Listen carefully to your teacher's directions for completing this exercise.

BACK TO BACK DICTATION

STUDENT A

Smallpox was

> a. on the world's deadliest disease list.
> b. one of the world's deadliest diseases.
> c. one of our world's most deadliest diseases.

The disease, considered so common 30 years ago,

> a. in effect bothered 10 and 15 million patients **each year.**
> b. had an effect by 10 and 15 million places **each year.**
> c. infected between 10 and 15 million people **each year.**

It was caused

> a. by false starts
> b. by the iris
> c. by a virus

that spread from **person to person**

through the air,

> a. and there was no treatment for it.
> b. in that there was no treatment for it.
> c. had there been treatments for it.

It spread across the human population

> a. caused a million of deaths.
> b. covered millions of deaths
> c. causing millions of deaths.

It left millions of others scarred and blinded.

BACK TO BACK DICTATION

STUDENT A

> a. Smallpox has gone down in history books
> b. Smallpox has gone down into the history books
> c. Smallpox is gone down in history books.

as being the first disease ever

> a. to be faced by humans.
> b. to be erased by humans.
> c. to be the first of humans.

A worldwide vaccination program

> a. had been widened it out by 1978
> b. had wiped it out by 1978
> c. had whipped it up by 1978

and in May 1980, the World Health Organization,

> a. had urgency in the United Nations,
> b. and a gentle offer of the United Nations,
> c. an agency of the United Nations,

formally announced that smallpox

> a. had been totally eliminated.
> b. had been officially limited.
> c. had been widely illuminated.

As a result,

> a. vaccination throughout the world
> b. vaccination around the world
> c. vaccination allowed the world

stopped.

BACK TO BACK DICTATION

STUDENT B

a. Short marks have
b. Smallpox was
c. A small part is

one of the world's deadliest diseases.

a. The disease was considered so common 30 years ago,
b. The disease was a common concern of people 30 years ago,
c. The disease, considered so common 30 years ago,

infected between 10 and 15 million people each year.

a. It is a clause
b. It has a cause
c. It was caused

by a virus

a. that spread from person to person through the air,
b. that sprayed from person to person through there,
c. that's bread from person to person forever.

and there was no treatment for it.

a. He speared across the human population
b. These tread across the human population
c. It spread across the human population

causing millions of deaths.

a. It left millions of others scarred and blinded.
b. It left over millions scared and blotted.
c. It's like millions that are scarred and branded.

Smallpox has gone down in history books

a. as beginning the fourth disease ever
b. as being the first disease ever
c. has been the first disease forever

to be erased by humans.

BACK TO BACK DICTATION

STUDENT B

a. A world of wide vaccination program
b. I wondered why a vaccination program
c. A world wide vaccination program

had wiped it out by 1978

a. as in May 1918 the World Health Organization,
b. and in May 1980 the World Health Organization,
c. add in May 1980 the Organization of World Health,

an agency of the United Nations,

a. from all the announced short marks
b. forgo the announcement that small parts
c. formally announced that smallpox

had been totally eliminated.

a. As a result
b. And the result
c. Add a result

vaccination throughout the world

a. stopped.
b. strapped.
c. stabbed.

RAPID REPLY – PART I

Write answers to these questions.

1. Circle the answer which is **not** true.
   a. Smallpox killed many people.
   b. It was a common disease 30 years ago.
   c. Smallpox could be treated if discovered early.
   d. Smallpox was caused by a virus.

2. Millions of people died as a result of contracting smallpox. What two other effects did smallpox have on the people who got it?

   _____ and _____.

3. How was smallpox wiped out? _____

   _____.

4. In what year did the World Health Organization announce that smallpox no longer existed. _____

Co-operActivity

FINISH THE STORY

Read the rest of the story about smallpox, paragraph by paragraph. In other words, you will read one paragraph silently and then stop. You and a partner will have a few minutes to help each other understand the paragraph's contents. When you have finished, read the next paragraph silently and stop again, so you and your partner can confirm each other's understanding of that paragraph. Follow the same procedure until you have read the whole story.

REALLY, REALLY GETTING RID OF SMALLPOX

Keeping viruses alive

THE UNITED NATIONS BUILDING, NY—Smallpox was one of the world's deadliest diseases. The disease, considered so common 30 years ago, infected between 10 and 15 million people each year. It was caused by a virus that spread from person to person through the air, and there was no treatment for it. It spread across the human population causing millions of deaths. It left millions of others scarred and blinded.

Smallpox has gone down in history books as being the first disease ever to be erased by humans. A worldwide vaccination program had wiped it out by 1978 and in May 1980, the World Health Organization (WHO), an agency of the United Nations, formally announced that smallpox had been totally eliminated. As a result, vaccination throughout the world stopped.

But the virus that causes smallpox is still alive, that is, in medical laboratories. Remaining samples of the virus are being stored in labs in the United States and Russia, and there is now disagreement over whether those samples should be destroyed. The WHO is advising that the virus be destroyed by June 30, 1999. Actually, the WHO had advised destroying the virus twice before — once in 1993 and once in 1995. Each time, however, scientists protested, saying that the virus might be important for future research.

Some experts say that when storing viruses such as smallpox in a lab, there is the constant danger of the virus escaping or being stolen. Others say that the danger is outweighed by the possible benefits for scientific research. Virologists have used viruses for such purposes as insect control, cell research, and the development of vaccines and other drugs.

The WHO claims that it has already done some work on the smallpox virus. It has made maps of the virus' structure and has cloned parts of the virus that don't cause infection.

The final decision to destroy the virus must be made by the U.S. and Russia.

HELPFUL VOCABULARY

infect – give someone a disease

virus – something that causes infectious illness: the common cold virus

scar – have or be given a permanent mark on your skin

vaccination – protection against a disease with a safe form of the virus that causes the disease

wipe out – completely remove

agency – an organization or department (usually within a government) that has a specific responsibility

eliminate – get rid of

stored – kept

traditional sit-up – (exercise) lying on the back, a person sits up without moving the legs, in order to strengthen stomach muscles

modified sit-up – (exercise) as above, but with knees bent

protest – complain strongly
constant – happening regularly or all the time
outweigh – more important or valuable than something else
benefit – advantage
virologist – someone who studies viruses
cell – the smallest part of an animal or plant that can exist on its own (red and white blood cells)
clone – copy (a gene) artificially in a science laboratory

RAPID REPLY – PART II

Write answers to these questions about the remaining paragraphs of the article on smallpox. Check your answers with your partner.

5. Where exactly is the smallpox virus being kept?

_____

6. How many times has the WHO tried to have the virus destroyed? _____

7. What was the scientists' argument for not destroying the virus?

_____

8. Circle the best answer. Paragraph 4 talks mainly about

   a. ideas behind virologists' research

   b. two opposing views concerning the destruction of the smallpox virus

   c. developing benefits of vaccines and other drugs in laboratories

9. What was the WHO's purpose for making maps of the virus' structure?

_____

10. Finish this sentence:

The destruction of the smallpox virus must _____

_____

A CLOSER LOOK

1. List the five most important details of the article here.

   a.

   b.

   c.

   d.

   e.

Do you and your classmates agree?

2. Imagine that you are the reporter who wrote this newspaper article. Write a headline that you think would attract readers to your story.

_____

3. Discussion. Together with your group, review the article on smallpox to list the **PROS** (reasons for) and **CONS** (reasons against) of destroying the remaining samples of the smallpox virus.

PROS	CONS
1.	1.
2.	2.
3.	3.
4.	4.

- Discuss these questions:
    a. From the information in the article, which reasons were easier to find - pros or cons?
    b. Do you think the article gives a balanced view of the subject?
    c. Explain to your group why you are either for or against the destruction of the smallpox virus.

CLASS EXERCISES

- **Quick-Write.** A quick-write is a chance to write without stopping to make corrections.

    You wake up sick and realize you have a big test in class today. Write a letter to your teacher explaining why you can't come to class to take the test. Give lots of details about how sick you are. You have 3 minutes. Go!

    _____

    _____

    _____

    _____

    _____

    _____

- **Take The Health Test.** Guess the answers to the questions below to see how much you know. (Answers are at the end of this chapter. **Don't peek** until you have finished.)

1. (**T-F**) Frozen vegetables are not as healthy as fresh.

2. Which US Department (government office) is responsible for carefully checking the quality of the foods we buy?

    _____

3. (**T-F**) Cold, wet weather increases your chance of catching a cold.

4. About how many hairs fall out of your head every day? _____

5. What should you do before you begin any physical activity? _____

6. (**T-F**) You should brush your teeth after every meal.

7. There is an average of _____% sugar contained in most children's breakfast cereals which you buy in the supermarket.

8. How many calories can you burn cheering at a football game? _____

9. (**T-F**) In the United States, children younger than 12 years old must sit in the back seat while riding in a car.

10. Which vitamin is said to prevent colds? _____

11. (**T-F**) Traditional sit-ups are dangerous.

12. How many calories are there in a fast food cheeseburger? _____

13. (**T-F**) Reading in a room with dim lighting is harmful to your eyesight.

14. _____

(Make up a health question of your own to test your classmates.)

• In pairs or in a group, discuss these questions.

Do/Did you like studying science in school?
If you were a scientist, what kind of research would you like to do?
Do you think medical researchers will find a cure for cancer?, AIDS?
What are some major medical problems facing your country today?

Co-operActivity

SITUATION ROLE-PLAY

Your group can choose one of the following situations to write a very short dialog. Decide what characters you need, and then talk about what each character will say. Discuss the beginning, middle and end of the scenario before you actually write down the dialog. Your group will be asked to act it out in front of the class. It is not necessary for you to memorize your lines.

1. You are visiting a friend who is in the hospital with a broken leg. He/she is in a lot of pain. You have come to cheer him/her up.

2. A student starts to cry in the cafeteria. What happened? Try to help him/her.

3. Your friend gets stung by a bee directly on the eyelid. Help him/her walk to class.

4. A man is lying in a room on a hospital bed with bandages from head to toe. A doctor and nurse are also in the room. What happened?

Answers to the Health Test

1. False. Frozen vegetables are likely to be fresher and more nutritious than supermarket produce transported across the country. 2. The United States Department of Agriculture. 3. False. Weather conditions don't weaken your defenses against the common cold. 4. 100 (accept plus or minus 20) 5. **Warm up.** 6. False. It takes 16-24 hours for plaque to develop. Brushing your teeth twice a day is enough. 7. 51% (accept plus or minus 5%) 8. 250 (accept plus or minus 50 calories) 9. True. 10. Vitamin C 11. True. Traditional sit-ups can strain your back. Modified sit-ups are much safer. 12. 570 (accept plus or minus 30 calories) 13. False. Reading in dim light may cause eye strain but won't damage your eyes.

CHAPTER 6
A Pilot's Bill of Rights

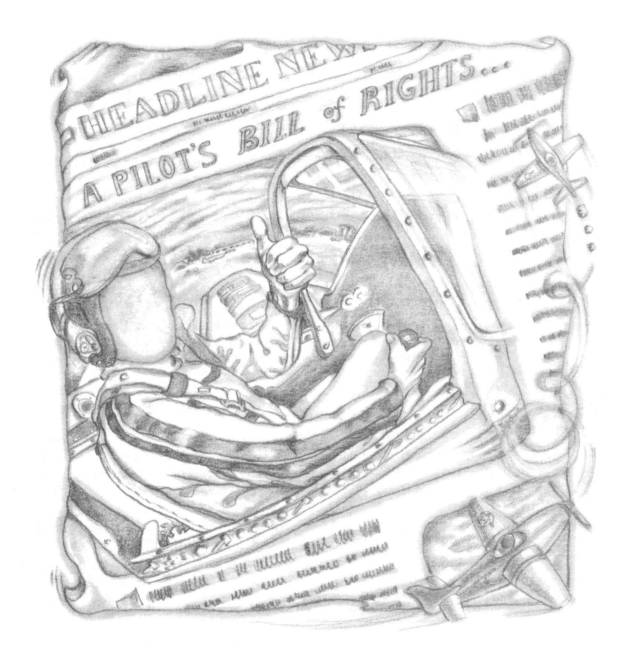

WARM-UP
Co-operActivity
SEND THE MESSENGER!

Your teacher will place a copy of the story's first paragraph a small distance away from your seat. You and a partner will write down the paragraph using the messenger-scribe method. You will be either a messenger or a scribe. The messenger approaches the paragraph as many times as is necessary to relay the whole paragraph to the scribe. The scribe writes down what the messenger says. To be the first one finished, you and your partner must have the paragraph written with perfect spelling and punctuation.

- Draw A Face. After you have completed the warm-up activity, use the illustration of the faceless man to draw what you think Bob Hoover looks like. Make your facial drawing as detailed as possible.

Co-operActivity

A PERSONAL WEB PAGE

Bob Hoover wants to find the woman of his dreams. Before you read the story, use your imagination to create a personal web page for Bob to be included in a dating service file. You may include information about his career, his experience as a pilot, his personality, his likes and dislikes, the kind of woman he wants to marry, his future plans etc. You may decorate or write up the page any way you like. Do this activity with a partner, and be prepared to explain why you made your choices for his web page.

BOB HOOVER'S PERSONAL WEB PAGE

- Continue reading the story, paragraph by paragraph with a partner.

A Pilot's Bill of Rights

Age discrimination

WASHINGTON, D. C., April, 1993 — All eyes stared. The pilot of the twin-engine plane turned off both his engines at 3,500 feet in the air. Not a person watching moved as the single-pilot airplane started to nose-dive towards the ground. It seemed well past the last possible moment, but then, Bob Hoover flipped his airplane and shot upward into the clouds. After a few more twists and somersaults, he glided his airplane to a perfect landing, and the crowd of people cheered. That's what happened the last time Bob Hoover, one of the greatest living pilots, performed his almost impossible stunts at the Oklahoma City air show. Two years later, he was told he would no longer be allowed to fly. Here's what happened.

Two of the onlookers at the air show that day were from the Federal Aviation Administration (FAA), a government agency in charge of air safety. (The FAA sends inspectors to all air shows.) They watched 72 year-old Bob Hoover pilot his plane, and it appeared to them that he seemed unsure of his maneuvers. They reported their findings to the administration, who then decided that Bob Hoover should have a physical examination. He did, and he passed it. Still, the FAA was not satisfied. They selected another set of doctors who concluded that Hoover was unfit to fly.

Hoover, a retired Air Force pilot, has been performing in air shows annually since 1940. "It's ridiculous!," Hoover told reporters. "I flew flawlessly." And his fellow air show pilots agree: they have gathered together to raise $50,000 to help with Hoover's legal costs, saying that the FAA is guilty of age discrimination.

The FAA says that Hoover has neurological problems. They reported that problem-solving tests took him three times longer than average. Doctors also said that his bulb-shaped red nose could be a result of heavy drinking. According to the test results and the FAA medical standards, they decided that Hoover's medical condition disqualified him from flying. Bob Hoover was grounded.

Hoover has said that the test results show nothing about his ability to fly. He recalls one test that lasted six hours in which he was asked to continuously repeat lists of words. And as far as his red nose is concerned, Hoover can prove he has had surgery on his nose many times to remove skin cancer.

Former super test pilot, General Charles "Chuck" Yeager, who in 1947 was the first pilot to break the sound barrier with Bob Hoover following him in a "chase" plane, describes his friend's flying as "perfect." And Hoover got his own group of doctors, who stated that he was physically fit to fly.

HELPFUL VOCABULARY

twin-engine plane – an airplane with two engines

nose dive – the nose (front end) of the plane pointing to the ground

somersault – the action of rolling forward until your feet go over your head and touch the ground again

stunt – a dangerous action that is done to entertain people

onlookers – people who watch something without being involved in it

in charge of – in control of; responsible for

maneuvers – skillful moves

annually – every year

flawlessly – with no mistakes

fellow – relating to people who do the same thing you do

guilty – having done a crime

neurological – relating to the brain and nervous system

standard – acceptable level of quality, skill, or ability

disqualify – stop someone from taking part in an activity or competition usually because s/he has done something wrong

grounded – an airplane or pilot who is not allowed to continue flying
recalls – remembers
surgery – medical treatment in which a doctor cuts open your body to fix, change or remove something inside
former – having a particular position before, but not now

RAPID REPLY

Write answers to these questions immediately.

1. In what city did the air show take place? _____

2. Why did the airplane start to nose-dive towards the ground?

_____

3. Why did the FAA administration request that Bob Hoover have a physical examination? _____

_____

4. What was Bob Hoover's reaction to the FAA request?
    a. surprise
    b. anxiety
    c. disagreement

5. How old is Bob Hoover? _____

6. (T-F) Bob Hoover was given a problem-solving test that took him twice as long to complete as the average person.

7. The FAA thought Bob was a heavy drinker because
    a. he did twists and somersaults with his airplane.
    b. he had a big red nose.
    c. he had been an Air Force pilot.

8. Bob Hoover is suing the FAA for _____ discrimination.

A CLOSER LOOK

1. Look at the title of the story. What do you think it means?

_____

2. List the three most important details of the story here.
    a.

    b.

    c.

Do you and your classmates agree?

3. Imagine that you are the reporter who wrote this newspaper article. Write a headline that you think would attract readers to your story.

_____

4. The paragraph below has been taken directly from the story.
Fill in the missing words **without referring to the story**. You may work with a partner.

Two of the onlookers _____ the air show that day _____ from the Federal Aviation Administration (_____). They watched 72 _____-old Bob Hoover pilot his _____, and it appeared to _____ that he seemed _____ about his maneuvers. They _____ their findings to the administration, _____ then decided that Bob Hoover should have a physical _____.

CLASS EXERCISES

- In small groups, discuss these questions.

  What was the best about being a child? What was the worst?
  What will be the best about getting older? What will be worst?
  What is the ideal age?

  Discuss whether or not you think the FAA is guilty of age discrimination. Use the facts from the story to help form your opinion.

  Do you think Bob Hoover can win his case?
  Write your opinion in the space below.

  _____

  _____

  _____

  _____

  _____

Co-operActivity

INTERVIEW A CLASSMATE

Find out about discrimination in his/her country. You may ask the following questions.

1. Is there a group of people who are discriminated against?

   _____

2. Circle the reason(s) for the discrimination.

   nationality   language   religion   sex   age   occupation

   region   skin color   (other) _____

3. Is the government doing anything to stop the discrimination?

   _____

4. Do you think the situation has any chance of changing in the future?

   Yes/No, because _____

CHAPTER 7

Troubled Waters

WARM-UP *Co-operActivity: MAKING PREDICTIONS FROM THE END*

Read the paragraph below. It is the last paragraph of a story. In pairs or in a group, try to guess what the story is about.

PORTOLA, California, March 22, 1997—If the state continues with the plan, 70% of the lake will be emptied out and then, the poison will be added. The idea is that the smaller the lake, the less poison necessary and the less costly the plan. The treatment will cost about $1.5 million. State officials estimate that the entire operation...will take about five years. They are sure they can do a good job.

Co-operActivity

STORY RELAY-RACE

You will participate as a "runner" in a story relay-race to find out about the problem facing the town of Portola, California. The class will be divided into several teams. Each team sends a runner to the teacher to get part of the story, and that runner then relays that part to the rest of the team. The team rotates its runners until it has the whole story. All teams play at the same time, and the group that works the fastest to complete the task wins. Please choose a team name before you begin the race. Good luck, and may the best team win!

Team Name:

TROUBLED WATERS

An environmental question

PORTOLA, California, March 22, 1997— Portola, California is a tiny mountain town surrounded by rocky canyons and grassy meadows. Tourists can enjoy the smell of thick forest pine as they fish for trout in the calm waters of Lake Davis. Sounds like a great place for a relaxing vacation, doesn't it? (Especially if you'd like to go fishing.) But, there is one mistake in the town's description. Lake Davis is now filled with northern pike, not trout, and the pike have created a big problem for the people of Portola and the State of California. Here's why.

State officials want to poison Lake Davis, which provides most of the drinking water for the people of Portola. All the fish must be killed, they say, in order to protect the salmon that live 100 miles away up the river. Pike, which are aggressive fish that eat everything in their path, were brought to Lake Davis illegally in the early 1990's. If they are not destroyed, they will escape, swim up the river and begin to eat the already decreasing populations of salmon.

According to Patrick O'Brian, a fishery biologist, the number of trout caught in Lake Davis has dropped by 40%. In three more years, he says, there won't be any trout left. O'Brian agrees that the lake must die in order to live. But O'Brian, who is from a small town himself, knows that the people of Portola think that big city government doesn't understand small town life.

Portola residents have a lot to worry about. Lake Davis attracts many tourists and sport fishermen which, in turn, provides jobs for the residents. David Takahashi owns a local convenience store and makes his living renting campsites and selling fishing equipment. He and other residents are afraid of what will happen to the town's drinking water, their tourist industry and the local economy if state officials go ahead with their plan to poison the lake. "Portola is a pristine place," says one of the residents interviewed by reporters, "and there aren't too many other places like this. How will we survive?"

State officials strongly believe that their plan to poison the lake is the only answer, and that the alternatives offered by the local residents, such as emptying the lake completely or fishing out all the pike (It is against the law to catch pike!) won't work. Also, pike are a strong fish, and government officials worry that if the pike are caught they will be carried away and put in other waters.

The officials say that they will use "rotenone," a chemical which is made from a tropical plant found in South America. They say the rotenone will disappear from the water supply within weeks and will not hurt the residents or forest animals that use the lake for drinking water. In addition, they plan to monitor some of the city wells for a month afterwards to be sure they are chemical-free. The state has also offered other water supplies for use by the residents during the treatment, although no dates have been scheduled.

County Supervisor Fran Roudebush is not happy about the state's plan to monitor some of the wells in the area. When interviewed by reporters, she said, "Would you want to be using one of the wells that wasn't being monitored?" She also refers to studies that show that rotenone and other chemicals that would be put in the water are carcinogens (substances known to cause cancer).

If the state continues with the plan, 70% of the lake will be emptied out and then, the poison will be added. The idea is that the smaller the lake, the less poison necessary and the less costly the plan. The treatment will cost about $1.5 million. State officials estimate that the entire operation, to get rid of the pike and add new trout will take about five years. They are sure they can do a good job.

Other Information
- The type of salmon referred to in the article is on the endangered species list.
- David Takahashi is now trying to sell his shop.
- An 18-inch pike was caught and opened up. There was a 12-inch trout inside.

HELPFUL VOCABULARY

canyon – a deep, low area between mountains
meadow – a field with wild grass and flowers
pine – an evergreen tree with needle-like leaves
poison – something that can kill you or make you sick
aggressive – forceful; always ready to attack
path – the direction or line along which something moves
illegal – not allowed by the law
biologist – someone who studies living things
provide – give or supply something to someone
local – within the area
residents – people who live in a certain area or house or apartment
convenience – ease of use
make a living – earn money to live on
economy – organization of a country's money, business, products
officials – people with responsible positions in an organization
pristine – extremely clean and almost unused
alternative – instead of
offer – say that you are willing to do something
monitor – carefully watch something over a period of time
treatment – a method designed to cure a sickness
estimate – say how much something will probably cost

RAPID REPLY

Write answers to these questions immediately.

1. Why do tourists come to Portola? _____

    _____

2. Lake Davis is now filled with northern pike, not _____

3. The two parties arguing about the lake are:
    a. the townspeople and the city of Portola
    b. the fishery biologists and the state officials
    c. Portola residents and the state government

4. The northern pike are a threat to the salmon that live **upstream because**

    _____

5. Paragraph 3 implies that Patrick O'Brian is for/against poisoning the lake.

6. What three things do Portola residents worry about if the state goes ahead with poisoning the lake?

    a. _____

    b. _____

    c. _____

7. (**T-F**) Rotenone comes from a plant that grows in cold temperatures.

8. How will the state officials be sure that residents will not drink poisoned water? _____

9. According to the information in paragraph 7, is Fran Roudebush for/ against poisoning Lake Davis?

10. The entire program for poisoning the lake will take _____ years.

A CLOSER LOOK

1. Look at the title of the story. What do you think it means?

    _____

2. List the three most important details of the story here.

    a.

    b.

    c.

    Do you and your classmates agree?

3. Imagine that you are the reporter who wrote this newspaper article. Write a headline that you think would attract readers to your story.

    _____

Co-operActivity

THE MOST FOR/THE MOST AGAINST

Together with your group, review the article on the problem in Portola to list the reasons for and the reasons against poisoning Lake Davis. There are many for each side. See if your group can find the most!

FOR	AGAINST
1.	1.
2.	2.
3.	3.
4.	4.
5.	5.
6.	6.
7.	7.
8.	8.
9.	9.
10.	10.

Co-operActivity

VOCABULARY THROUGH PICTURES

You will need 1 blank sheet of paper for this activity. Fold the paper in half horizontally. Counting the front and back sides of the paper, you should have 4 equal parts or boxes.

Now, choose 4 vocabulary words from the Helpful Vocabulary list and quickly draw a picture of each in one of the 4 boxes. The teacher will collect all the drawings and hold each one up in front of the class for viewing. Shout out the vocabulary word you think is being represented in the drawing.

CLASS EXERCISES

- In small groups, discuss your opinions about the question below.

  According to your list of reasons for and against poisoning Lake Davis, should the state go ahead with its plan?

  After the discussion, write and support your final decision here.

  _____

  _____

  _____

  _____

  _____

  _____

  If you were one of the state officials, would your final decision be the same as the one you wrote above?

  Yes/No, because _____

  _____

  If you were a Portola resident, would your final decision be the same as the one you wrote above?

  Yes/No, because _____

  _____

- Here is a list of some environmental problems facing us today. With a partner or in small groups, name the 3 biggest problems. Which of these environmental problems do you know the most about?

____ **Smog**	____ **Sewage Waste**	____ **Pesticides**
____ **Acid Rain**	____ **Solid Waste** (paper, plastics, cans etc.)	
____ **Oil Spills**	____ **Greenhouse Effect**	____ **Noise Pollution**

DICTATION

Your teacher will dictate a passage to you three times at a natural speed. The first time you hear the passage, listen for the general meaning. The second time you hear the passage, you will have a chance to write down what you hear in the space below. Listen to the passage again for the third time, so you can check what you wrote and make any necessary changes or additions.

_____

_____

_____

_____

_____

_____

_____

_____

_____

_____

Now check your dictation with paragraph 2 of the story.

Co-operActivity

GIVING DIRECTIONS

With your teacher's guidance, you and your team are going to help a class representative draw an exact copy of a city map by giving very detailed directions (instructions). Feel free to tell the class representative to redraw something if you are not satisfied with the way it looks. For example, if a line is too long, ask him/her to redraw it to make it shorter. Likewise, if a shape is too narrow, ask him/her to make the shape wider. The team whose picture makes the more exact copy wins.

CHAPTER 8

A Long, Long Time Ago…

WARM-UP

In pairs or in a group, discuss these questions.

Do you like to talk about politics? Why or why not?

What qualities should a politician have?

Does your country have a president?

Would you like to be president? (of your country? of the US?)

If you had a high political position, name one situation in your country you would try to change.

Co-operActivity

GUESS THE FACTS

Read these statements to get the facts of the story. Three statements are false; the rest are true. Work with a partner to decide which statements are false. After you have finished, meet with another pair of students to compare your answers. You should be able to tell why you chose the false statements you did. When you have finished, your teacher will tell you which statements are the false. Ask your teacher any yes/no questions to help make the false statements true.

GUESS THE FACTS

_____ a. John Mazziotti is the mayor of a growing city in Florida.

_____ b. It was difficult for him to become the mayor.

_____ c. John Mazziotti sold drugs to an undercover policeman.

_____ d. John went to jail.

_____ e. Mazziotti never graduated from his university.

_____ f. He married a policewoman and had three children.

_____ g. He became the owner of a hardware store.

_____ h. While in Florida, John became interested in politics.

_____ i. He became mayor but still works at the hardware store.

_____ j. John earns $8,000 a year as mayor of his city.

_____ k. John Mazziotti has been a good citizen his whole life.

_____ l. John wants to build a community center for his city.

A LONG, LONG TIME AGO...

Crime and politics

PALM BAY, Fla.,March, 1997— John Mazziotti is the mayor of Palm Bay, a growing city in central Florida. He is a mayor with an unusual history because he is a convicted criminal. What is even more unusual is the fact that the people of Palm Bay voted for him over 3 other candidates knowing that he had spent time in prison for selling an ounce (16 grams) of marijuana to an undercover policeman. Here is John Mazziotti's story.

After Mazziotti left prison in 1974, he enrolled in a community college and later graduated from Pennsylvania State University with a degree in business administration. He married a schoolteacher and together they raised two daughters. He moved to Florida in the mid-1980's, sold real estate for a while and then opened up a hardware store. He became involved in local politics and was elected to the City Council. He did an excellent job as a council member, and in 1995, he was elected mayor of Palm Bay — a part-time job that pays $8,000 a year. He still works half-days at the hardware store.

Mazziotti told reporters, "The voters recognized that what happened to me, happened a long time ago."

But the story does not end here because Mazziotti's political opponents soon discovered that there was more to know about this newly-elected mayor. Mayor Mazziotti has now announced that in 1972 he also went to jail for more than two years for selling amphetamines and importing drugs across the Canadian border.

The people of Palm Bay have different opinions about Mazziotti. Some see him as a man who made mistakes in the past but was able to turn his life around. Other residents of Palm Bay are not so forgiving. They say Mazziotti can't be trusted because he didn't tell the people everything about his criminal record. "We were willing to overlook the marijuana incident," one woman, who worked on his campaign, told reporters. "But he lied about the other things. He is an embarrassment to the community. He should resign."

- Should Mazziotti have told the "whole" story of his criminal past?
- Should Mazziotti still be mayor of Palm Bay?

Mazziotti would just like to continue to concentrate on his mayoral goals to set up a second community center and improve the city's water drainage system. He said he didn't talk about his complete record before the election because no one asked. "I don't walk down the street with a sign saying, 'I'm an ex-con,'" he told reporters. "For 20 years I've been a good citizen."

HELPFUL VOCABULARY

mayor – a person elected to lead the government of a town or city

convicted – found guilty of a crime in a court of law

candidate – someone who is seeking a position

undercover – acting secretly in order to catch criminals or find out information

real estate – the business of selling buildings or land

hardware – materials or equipment you use in your home

local – relating to a particular nearby place or area

council – a group of people who are elected as part of a town or city government

opponents – people on opposite sides of a contest or argument

amphetamines – pills that keep you awake

turn one's life around – make changes in your life to fix the problems

residents – people who live in a place such as a house or an apartment

overlook – not notice or pay attention to

incident – an event or happening

embarrassment – shame

resign – leave a job or position voluntarily

goal – a successful end result

drainage – the direction water flows; often a system of underground pipes

ex-con – (con = convict) someone who once had to spend time in jail for committing a crime

RAPID REPLY

Write answers to these questions immediately.

1. John Mazziotti is mayor of _____.

2. Which statement is **not** true. Mazziotti won the race for mayor

    a. and had little difficulty winning.

    b. in an election with three other candidates.

    c. even though the people knew he had gone to jail for selling marijuana.

    d. but did not accept the position.

3. (**T-F**) John Mazziotti transferred from a community college to a university to get his degree in business administration.

4. Did John do well as a city council member in Florida? Yes/No

    People said he _____

5. What jobs did John have before he became mayor?

    _____

6. Paragraphs 6 and 7 discuss _____

    _____

    _____

    _____

7. John Mazziotti didn't tell about his complete criminal record because

    a. no one asked

    b. he was ashamed

    c. he felt he did nothing wrong

A CLOSER LOOK

1. Look at the title of the story. What do you think it means?

    _____

2. List the three most important details of the story here.

    a.

    b.

    c.

    Do you and your classmates agree?

Co-operActivity

BUILDING A WORD DOMAIN

The class will be divided into groups for this activity. The word "city" has been written in a bubble on the board, one time for each group. Each group is in charge of one "city" bubble. Your group is responsible for trying to associate as many words as possible with the word "city". Each of you will look at the word "city" for a few moments, and then write the first city-related word that pops into your mind in a bubble offshoot, for example 'crowds' or 'downtown'. **Be sure to always refer back to the word "city" every time you add a bubble offshoot with a related word.** Continue taking turns at the board to add as many bubble offshoots as possible. See which group has the most word relationships.

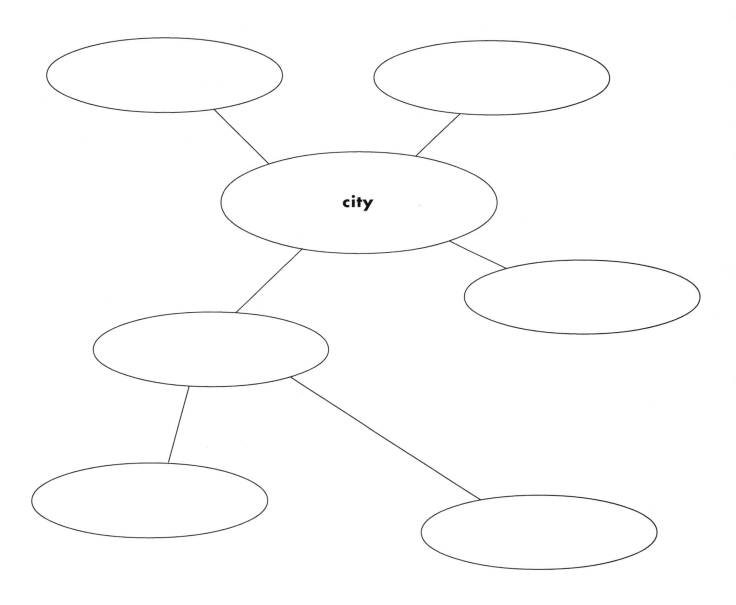

CLASS EXERCISES

The following activities may be done in small groups or in pairs.

- The residents of Palm Bay have opposite opinions about John Mazziotti. In small groups, make a list of the reasons why some residents might believe he has turned his life around and why some residents might believe he can't be trusted. Refer to the story at any time during the discussion. Use the workspace below to write down your group's ideas.

Mazziotti *Should* be Mayor	Mazziotti *Shouldn't* be Mayor

Co-operActivity

*DEBATE**

Your teacher is going to help conduct a class debate. Decide if you are for or against John Mazziotti's continuation as mayor of Palm Bay.

* In a formal debate, the same number of people must speak for each side. They have the right to reply directly to the speaker on the opposite side. Speakers "for" and "against" usually take turns, and all of the speeches are limited in time. With informal debates, there is often no time limit for speeches, and the number of people on each side may be unequal.

- How does this story compare with the story about 42 year-old Michael Maynard, the school teacher who was fired for a marijuana drug arrest when he was 20 years old. (See "Up In Smoke")

- What do you think will happen to John Mazziotti? Write your answer in the space below.

_____

_____

_____

_____

_____

_____

Co-operActivity

BINGO

Below is a bingo card with 8 boxes and a free space. Choose 8 words from the Helpful Vocabulary list and write one word in each box in pencil. Your teacher will read a vocabulary word's meaning out loud. If you have the word on your card that matches that meaning, **x** out the box. The teacher will continue to read meanings from the Helpful Vocabulary list. As soon as you have 3 boxes "**x**"ed out either horizontally or vertically shout "Bingo!"

	FREE	

CHAPTER 9

Got a Cigarette?

WARM-UP

Co-operActivity

INTRODUCTION CLOZE

Work with a partner to fill in the blanks of the story's first paragraph. You may use as many words in the blank as you like.

Jean Connor began _____ in 1961 when she

was 15 years old. As she got older, she became _____

_____. In 1993, she was told _____

_____. In 1995, she

died of it. She was 49 years old and _____

_____.

Now compare your answers with another pair of students. Be prepared to support the reason(s) for your fill-ins. When you are finished, check the first paragraph of the story to see how closely you match it.

BONUS: What adjective is used in the first paragraph to describe what kind of smoker Jean Connor was?

Co-operActivity

QUESTION EXCHANGE

You and your group will read this story through a question exchange. Each group needs two sheets of paper for this activity. Your group will use one sheet of paper to write down comprehension questions and the other sheet to answer comprehension questions.

Your group will be given one or more of six paragraphs from the story. The group is responsible for reading and understanding the reading and making up at least three comprehension questions about it. One person from the group will write down the comprehension questions on one piece of paper entitled "Comprehension Questions For Paragraph (X)." Later on, these questions will be answered by other groups.

After you have written down the questions, give them to another group to answer. Your group will also receive a set of questions. Your group has to read the paragraph in the story that pertains to those questions, and answer those questions on your second sheet of paper. Continue the activity until your group has received and answered all the comprehension questions of all six paragraphs. Remember to use your group's second sheet of paper to answer all the comprehension questions you receive.

One by one, the groups will announce the answers to their original questions, for which they receive credit, while your group listens and tallies your correct answers. The group with the most correct answers wins. Good luck!

GOT A CIGARETTE?

The price of health

JACKSONVILLE, Florida, April, 1997—Jean Connor began smoking in 1961 when she was 15 years old. As she got older she became a two- to three-pack-a-day smoker. In 1993, Jean Connor was told she had lung cancer. In 1995, she died of it. She was 49 years old and the mother of three children.

Jean Connor's family is suing the R.J. Reynolds tobacco company. Her family says that the tobacco company did not show responsibility and tried to hide information about the dangers and addictiveness of smoking. The family's lawyer is Greg Maxwell.

According to Maxwell, Jean Connor's death was a slow, painful one. It was also very difficult for her family to watch her die. The family wants money from the company for Jean's death and for the pain and suffering her death caused the whole family.

Greg Maxwell and his team of lawyers will argue that R.J. Reynolds, the nation's second largest cigarette maker, never told Jean Connor and other smokers how to lessen the dangers of smoking, such as not smoking down to the butt, because there is more tar in the last few puffs. They will also argue that the company strongly advertised its product suggesting it was safe and, in fact, fashionable to smoke.

The team of lawyers is also planning to introduce R.J. Reynolds documents that show that the company knew smoking was addictive and dangerous long before warning labels came out in 1966. They will argue that by 1966, Jean Connor was already addicted to cigarettes.

Reynolds, however, says that it is not responsible for Jean Connor's smoking habit. The company says that Connor made a personal choice to smoke and knew of the possible dangers. Besides that, they say, Jean Connor changed cigarette brands in 1983 to Benson & Hedges, made by the Philip Morris Company. She had been smoking *that* brand for ten years when doctors diagnosed her lung cancer.

Greg Maxwell will argue that Jean Connor smoked the Reynolds brand of cigarette for more than 20 years. It was during that time when most of the damage was done to her lungs.

The Connor family chose not to sue the Philip Morris company in order to not complicate the case.

Did you know that...

- The team of lawyers hired by the Connor family have already won a $750,000 lawsuit against another tobacco company.
- The R.J. Reynolds Tobacco Company is a $50-billion industry.
- The U.S. tobacco industry employs more than 650,000 people.
- Twenty-three states have sued tobacco companies in an effort to get back billions of dollars in Medicaid (state-funded health care) costs for treating sick smokers.
- The tobacco industry agrees that cigarettes cause some health problems, but it disagrees that nicotine is addictive. The industry also says that it can't be proved that cigarettes cause cancer.
- Three former employees of the Philip Morris company have sworn that the company controlled nicotine levels to keep smokers addicted.
- A case in Texas brought the tobacco industry to court because its advertisements tried to attract children to smoking cigarettes.
- On January 18, 1998, the State of Texas won a $15.3 billion settlement against the big tobacco companies.
- A Florida court allowed airline flight attendants to sue tobacco companies for second-hand smoke-related health problems.
- According to the Department of Health Services, tobacco is the number one cause of preventable death in this country.
- About 50 million Americans still smoke despite label warnings first ordered by Congress more than 30 years ago.
- Tobacco companies now sell more cigarettes abroad than they do in the U.S.

HELPFUL VOCABULARY

lung – the organ in the body used for breathing

cancer – dangerous cell disease which may cause death

suing – taking someone to court to get money because that person did something wrong to you

habit – regular activity

cause – make happen

addictive – causes a habit to form

suffer – experience something bad

butt – end of a cigarette after most of it has been smoked

tar – the sticky material in cigarettes that makes your fingers brown and your lungs black

puff – a small breath of smoke or air

documents – official records

brand – type of product made by a specific company

diagnose – find what is wrong with a person

damage – bad effect or harm

complicate – make something more difficult or confusing

A CLOSER LOOK

1. List the three most important details of the story here.

   a.

   b.

   c.

   Do you and your classmates agree?

2. Imagine that you are the reporter who wrote this newspaper article. Write a headline that you think would attract readers to your story.

CLASS EXERCISES

- In pairs or in a group, discuss your opinions about the following questions.

  In your country:

  1. Is cigarette smoking popular?

  2. What kind of advertising is there for cigarette smoking?

  3. Has anything been done to limit places where people can smoke?

  4. Do you know anyone who smokes?

  5. Do you know anyone who has recently quit smoking?

  6. Do you think people can be hypnotized into quitting?

  7. In your opinion, why do you think young people start smoking?

8. Do you think the government should make laws about who can smoke and where they can smoke? After all, isn't smoking a personal freedom? (Write your opinion here after you have discussed the question with your group.)

_____

_____

_____

_____

_____

_____

_____

_____

_____

9. Do you think Jean Connor's family can win this case?

Yes or no?

Yes, because _____

_____

_____

_____

_____.

No, because _____

_____

_____

_____.

- **Quick-Write.** A quick-write is a chance to write without stopping to make corrections. Read the paragraph below.

On August 30, 1996 the widow of the "Marlboro Man" sued the tobacco industry for helping to cause the death of her husband, David McLean. He died of lung cancer, and his widow says it is because he had to regularly smoke as many as five packs of cigarettes a day while he was being photographed for magazine advertisements or filming TV commercials.

Write a letter to the Marlboro Man's widow in the space below to tell her how you feel. You have 5 minutes. Go!

Date: _____

_____,

_____

_____

_____

_____

_____

_____

_____

_____

_____

_____

_____

_____

_____.

Sincerely,

_____

Co-operActivity

ROLE-PLAY INTERVIEW

You and your partner will choose one character from the story. One of you will pretend to be a news reporter; the other, the chosen character. Prepare an emotional interview between the reporter and the character that you will present to the class. Be creative! There are many characters to choose from.

CHAPTER 10

Is Shakespeare Really Dead?

WARM-UP

In pairs or in a group, write a poem using all of the words in the box or as many as possible. You may repeat words if you wish. Share your poem with your classmates.

upon	might	hand	that
see	she	I	her
oh	cheek	a	glove
leans	were	touch	how

_____
_____
_____
_____
_____
_____
_____
_____
_____
_____
_____
_____.

Co-operActivity

PAIR DICTATION

You and a partner can find the missing information for the first paragraph of the article through pair dictation. You are either **Student Y**, page 56 or **Student Z**, page 60. Sit face-to-face with your partner. Look only at your paragraph page! Your partner has the missing information and must dictate to you so that you can fill in the blank spaces. Student Y starts by telling (dictating) the information to Student Z, who must fill in the blank. Then, Student Z tells (dictates) the missing information to Student Y, who also will fill in the blank. In other words, Students Y and Z will alternate dictating and filling in the blanks. Don't look at your partner's paragraph during the dictation. In the end, both you and your partner should have a completed version of the first paragraph of the story. Review the contents of the paragraph together.

When you finish, return to page 56 to continue this lesson.

STUDENT Y PAIR DICTATION

William Shakespeare (1564-1616) _____.

He is thought to be _____. His plays

have been performed _____. No

other writer has enjoyed _____,

admiration and affection.

Co-operActivity

PROS AND CONS

You and a partner have been assigned one paragraph from the rest of the story. Read your assigned paragraph to determine if you have a pro (for) or a con (against) point of view. You must understand your paragraph's point of view clearly and be able to explain it to others without reading word for word from the text. Remember to use the Helpful Vocabulary list.

PROS MEET PROS AND CONS MEET CONS

All students with pro paragraphs meet together to form one group. All the students with con paragraphs should do the same. Everyone in your group will share his/her paragraph's point of view and together you will build a strong defense for your side.

PROS MEET CONS

Change your group so you have a mixture of students with pro and con paragraphs. Your new group should have all the paragraphs of the story represented.

Summarize your paragraph's point of view for the new group and listen and take notes while your other group members summarize theirs. Then, as a group, discuss whether you agree or disagree with the ideas presented in each paragraph and the larger issue of student choice.

Is Shakespeare Really Dead?

The liberal vs. the conservative

LOS ANGELES, CA, March 25, 1997—William Shakespeare (1564-1616) was an English playwright and poet. He is thought to be the greatest writer of all time. His plays have been performed and read all over the world. No other writer has enjoyed such lasting and continued interest, admiration and affection. But times have changed. At Georgetown University in Washington, DC, the faculty has removed Shakespeare from its list of required authors for English majors and replaced him with more non-traditional courses such as "The Poetry of Music" and "Heroes in Science Fiction" that really attract student interest.

One recent study, mentioned by the Los Angeles Times, shows that two-thirds of the nation's top 70 universities no longer require that English majors study Shakespeare. But contemporaries say that the interest in Shakespeare is still strong, and that many students sign up for a Shakespeare class even though it is not a required course.

Conservative educators are furious. They think that Shakespeare is too important and that studying him should be a student requirement, not a student choice. Jerry Martin, president of an educational advisory committee in Washington asked reporters, "Would you not require an anatomy course in medical school because you think most students will take it anyway?"

One professor at Georgetown, who voted to exclude Shakespeare as a requirement, points out, "When it comes to culture, we often force people to read what we think will be good for them."

But Jerry Martin believes that a strong academic foundation is necessary for a generation raised on gangster films and television violence. He told interviewers that he wants to be sure that the schools are producing successful leaders for the 21st century.

Herbert Lindenberger, director of the Modern Language Association and professor of English and comparative literature at Stanford University believes that students shouldn't be forced to study Shakespeare. "At Stanford, where Shakespeare has never been a requirement," Lindenberger says, "students can learn about Shakespeare in lots of courses. "Even pop culture courses usually have a section on Shakespeare." he adds. Lindenberger believes the cultural studies courses that have been added for English majors are very exciting. "I'm proud to see people doing new things."

In fact, Sarah Loffler, an English major at Cal State Northridge, said she enrolled in two Shakespeare courses even though the university does not require English majors to take Shakespeare. "Whether or not it was a requirement wasn't the question." she told reporters. "It was a requirement I put on myself. Shakespeare is a must, just as in music you would say Mozart is a must." she added.

Benita Clark, a senior majoring in English at the same university, enrolled in a Shakespeare course but had to drop it within the first few weeks because she just had too many classes. "There are a lot of classes that I've missed because my schedule is too tight," she explained during an interview.

Many scholars congratulate the well-known University of California at Los Angeles. At UCLA's Westwood campus, English majors must take two Shakespeare courses, as well as courses on other classic English writers such as Milton and Chaucer.

Eric Sundquist, chairman of UCLA's English department feels that if most people agree Shakespeare is the greatest writer of the English language, then why not make students study his work. Sundquist does believe there is a place for more non-traditional courses, too. UCLA's English department offers classes in science fiction, gay and lesbian literature, children's books and Celtic mythology. "We want to have a good mix of opportunities for our students," he stated in his interview with reporters. Sundquist wants to give students a chance to study original work but, at the same time, give them a good foundation in British and American literature.

HELPFUL VOCABULARY

playwright – someone who writes plays
admiration – feeling of respect for someone
affection – feeling of gentle love and caring
faculty – all teachers of a school or college
tradition – ideas, habits etc., accepted for a long time
attract – make someone move towards something
top – best
contemporary – modern
conservative – not very modern; traditional
furious – very, very angry
advisory – for the purpose of giving advice

> **committee** – group of people chosen for a job or to make decisions
> **anatomy** – study of the human body
> **foundation** – base; idea; system
> **producing** – making something happen for a result or effect
> **serious** – sincere; true
> **drop a class** – withdraw from or officially stop taking a course
> **scholar** – someone who knows a lot about a certain subject
> **original** – completely new or different

RAPID REPLY

Write answers to these questions immediately.

1. Shakespeare was _____ when he died.

   a. in his sixties   c. in his fifties

   b. in his forties   d. in his thirties

2. Shakespeare was a playwright and a _____.

3. Paragraph 2 says that Georgetown University replaced the traditional Shakespeare with non-traditional courses because the professors thought

   a. Shakespeare should only be for English majors

   b. the courses would be more interesting to students

   c. the University should follow the other top schools

4. Why does Jerry Martin mention gangster films and television violence in paragraph 6? _____.

5. (**T-F**) Herbert Lindenberger thinks Shakespeare is not needed as a required course.

6. How many Shakespeare courses did Sarah Loffler take? _____

7. Does Sarah's university have Shakespeare as a requirement?

8. What is Benita Clark's problem?

   _____

   _____.

9. Which of these is **not** true about Eric Sundquist's opinion on Shakespeare courses for English majors?

   a. He wants Shakespeare to be a required course.

   b. He thinks non-traditional courses are equally important.

   c. He believes there can be a good foundation in literature even without Shakespeare.

   d. A good mix of courses is better than no mix at all.

A CLOSER LOOK

1. Look at the title of the story. What do you think it means?

   _____

2. List the six most important details of the story here.

   a.

   b.

   c.

   d.

   e.

   f.

   Do you and your classmates agree?

3. Imagine that you are the reporter who wrote this newspaper article. Write a headline that you think would attract readers to your story.

Co-operActivity

MEMORY CLOZE

Without looking back at the actual story, fill in the blanks for the following two paragraphs. You may need more than one word to fill in the blank. Work with a partner.

But Jerry Martin _____ that a strong academic foundation

is _____ for a generation raised on gangster _____

and television violence. He wants to be _____ that schools

are producing successful leaders _____ the 21st century.

Benita Clark, a senior majoring _____ English at the same

university, _____ in a Shakespeare course but had to drop

it _____ the first few weeks _____ she just had too

many classes. "_____ are a lot of classes that I've

_____ because my schedule is _____ tight," she

explained during an interview.

See how your answers compare with paragraphs 6 and 9 from the story. Did your answers also make sense?

CLASS EXERCISES

- In small groups, support your opinions about the questions below.

   1. Do you think English majors should be required to study Shakespeare?

   2. Do you think students should choose the courses for their major?

   3. Who chose your schedule of courses?

   4. Are you happy with your present schedule?

   5. What, if anything, would you like to change about your schedule?

Co-operActivity

THE 45-SECOND BOARD GAME

How much can you say in 45 seconds?

The board game below is played with three or four players. You will have 45 seconds in which to talk **non-stop** about the topic in your box. If you can't think of ideas, the other players in your group can help you by asking you questions about the topic.

a love story	free time	poetry		
		homework		
		dream job	tests	English grammar
				classmates
	a good book	a movie or a play	why study	getting to school

STUDENT Z PAIR DICTATION

_____ was an English playwright

and poet. _____ the greatest writer of

all time. _____ and read all

over the world. _____ such

lasting and continued interest, _____.

CHAPTER 11

Whose Child Is He, Anyway?

WARM-UP

In pairs or in a group, discuss the answers to these questions.

Do you have any memories of life at 4 years old?
As a child, what did you and your family do for fun?

Will (Did) you work less at your job to raise your children?
Will (Did) you want your spouse to work less?

WHOSE CHILD IS HE, ANYWAY?

A case of children's rights

CHICAGO, Illinois , May, 1991—Danny is almost four years old. He has lived his whole life with Kimberly and Jay Warburton, his adoptive parents. Danny is a happy, healthy, well-adjusted child.

Danny lives in a nice home in a suburb of Chicago. He enjoys playing with his 7-year-old brother, the Warburton's biological son. Danny's "father," 49, is a firefighter. His "mother," also in her forties, is a paralegal secretary.

But as Danny grows up with the Warburtons in the suburbs of Chicago, Otakar Kirchner, the boy's biological father, waits for Danny's return. Here's the story.

For the first 57 days of his child's life, Otakar Kirchner thought his son was dead. When Otakar learned that his son was not really dead but rather had been put up for adoption by his biological mother, Daniella, Otakar immediately claimed his rights as the boy's father and began a long, legal fight to get his son back. He called him Richard.

Otakar and Daniella, both originally from Czechoslovakia, met in the United States. They fell in love and began living together. But soon Otakar left Daniella to return to Czechoslovakia to take care of his dying grandmother. It was during that time that Daniella learned she was pregnant.

For some unclear reason, an aunt of Otakar telephoned Daniella and told her that Otakar had really returned to Czechoslovakia to marry an old girlfriend. Daniella was crushed. She had the baby, Richard. Then, believing that Otakar had left her for another woman, she decided to give baby Richard up for adoption. She hoped to give her son a chance for a good life. She sent word to Otakar Kirchner that she had given birth to his baby, but it died.

Otakar soon returned from Czechoslovakia and told Daniella that he still loved her. It was then that Daniella told him that Richard was alive and well, but that he had been adopted. As soon as Otakar was told that, they married, and he began his fight for legal parental rights to his son.

The court must now decide if the child should stay with his adoptive parents or begin a new life with his biological parents.

HELPFUL VOCABULARY

adopt – legally have someone else's child become yours
well-adjusted – able to deal with your problems and emotions
biological – relating to biology (the study of living things)
paralegal – someone whose job it is to help a lawyer
suburb – an area just outside a city where many people live
claimed – officially said
legal – allowed by law
crushed – feeling very sad, upset, shocked

Co-operActivity

SUMMARY EXCHANGE

You will need to summarize half the story and tell it to a partner.

First, the teacher will divide the class into two groups, and each group will read half the story. Group 1 will read paragraphs 1-4, group 2, paragraphs 5-8.

Next, you must read your assigned paragraphs and be able to answer the **Rapid Reply** questions for your part of the story. Check your answers with your group members to see if your answers are correct. If you're in Group 1, you should answer questions 1-6. If you're in group 2, answer questions 7-12. Also, remember to look at the "Helpful Vocabulary" list.

Once you have checked the **Rapid Reply** questions, quickly write down a summary of the information you read in the space provided, so you can tell your part of the story to a member of the opposite group.

Pair up with one student from the opposite group and take turns telling your part of the story. You may refer to your summary but don't read directly from it. Be sure to ask your partner questions if there is something you don't understand or if you want more information.

RAPID REPLY

Write answers to these questions immediately.

Group 1 Questions

1. In what city does Danny live? _____

2. Who are Kimberly and Jay Warburton? _____

3. In paragraph 2, the expression "in her forties" means

    a. She is forty years old.

    b. She will be forty years old.

    c. She is between forty and forty-nine years old.

4. Otakar Kirchner thought his son was _____.

5. (**T-F**) Daniella had a baby but did not keep it.

6. (**T-F**) When Otakar Kirchner found out his son was alive, he decided to move away from Chicago.

Group 1 Summary

_____

_____

_____

_____

Group 2 Questions

7. (**T-F**) Daniella and Otakar met and fell in love in Czechoslovakia.

8. Otakar told Daniella he had to return to Czechoslovakia because

_____

9. The aunt told Daniella that Otakar returned to Czechoslovakia because

_____

10. Daniella gave her baby up for adoption because

    a. she wasn't ready to have a baby yet.

    b. she wanted her baby to have a better life.

    c. the baby almost died.

11. (**T-F**) Otakar immediately decided to get his son back when he found out about the adoption.

12. What must the court decide? _____

_____

Group 2 Summary

_____

_____

_____

_____

A CLOSER LOOK

1. Look at the title of the story. What do you think it means?

_____

2. List the four most important details of the story here.

   a.

   b.

   c.

   d.

   Do you and your classmates agree?

3. Imagine that you are the reporter who wrote this newspaper article. Write a headline that you think would attract readers to your story.

_____

CLASS EXERCISES

- In small groups, discuss the answers to these questions.

   1. What do you know about the process of adoption?
   2. Do you know anyone who is adopted?
   3. Do you think an adopted a child should know his/her birth parents?
   4. Would you ever consider adopting a child?
   5. List the reasons for and against the following statements.

   The child should begin a new life with the Kirchners, his biological parents.

   Yes. a. _____

   b. _____

   c. _____

   d. _____

   e. _____

No. a. _____

b. _____

c. _____

d. _____

e. _____

The child should stay with the Warburtons, his adoptive parents.

Yes. a. _____

b. _____

c. _____

d. _____

e. _____

No. a. _____

b. _____

c. _____

d. _____

e. _____

Co-operActivity

A DETAILED IMAGE

Sit face-to-face with a partner. You will each need a blank sheet of paper for this activity. Fold the paper in half horizontally, and hold it as if it were a greeting card. You are only going to use the front and back sides of the "card". Choose a favorite relative, and draw a <u>detailed</u> picture of him/her on the front side. Write the title "My _____" (for example, "My Cousin") at the top. You may draw your relative's whole body or just the face. **Don't let anyone peek, especially your partner!**

When you have finished your drawing, turn your "card" over to the back side and pass it to your partner. Then, tell your partner what your relative looks like so that s/he may draw it on the back side of your paper. Remember to give many details in your description. Your partner will then describe his/her relative to you.

Finally, when you and your partner have finished drawing, exchange papers. See how well your partner's drawing resembles your favorite relative.

CHAPTER 12

Do You Believe…?

WARM-UP

Co-operActivity

SHARE A PICTURE

On a piece of paper, draw an alien with the following features. Add any other characteristics you like. Share your picture with a classmate. Then, tell about your alien's temperament and why it has come to Earth.

blood-shot eyes   a hairy nose   bony fingers   stocky feet

Co-operActivity

THE SENTENCE-COMPLETION GUESS

Below is a summary of the first two paragraphs of story about something mysterious that crashed in New Mexico in 1947. Work with a partner to fill-in the missing information with your best guesses. Then, read the story to see how close you are to the actual facts of the story.

One of the most famous stories in UFO history happened in 1947 when _____.

When the townspeople arrived at the scene, they saw _____

_____.

The military arrived at the site of the crash and announced

_____.

Within a few hours, the military announced that _____

_____. Since that day, no one has been allowed to see what the military took from the crash site.

Co-operActivity

READING ROLE-PLAY

You will be assigned one of the remaining paragraphs of the story. You and your group must read your assigned paragraph and act it out in "skit" form for the rest of the class. In this way, you can understand the contents of the entire story by listening to and watching fellow classmates "perform."

Do You Believe...?
The UFO cover-up

ROSWELL, New Mexico, June 14, 1947—One of the most famous stories in 'UFO' history happened 1947 when something mysterious crashed in the New Mexico desert near Roswell. When the townspeople arrived at the scene, they thought they saw dead and injured alien bodies. The military arrived at the desert site, announced that indeed a UFO had crashed near Roswell and quickly collected the wreckage.

Within a few hours, the military announced that what had crashed was nothing more than pieces of a hot-air weather balloon, not an alien spaceship. Since that day, no one has been allowed to see what the military took.

Many feel certain that the crash at Roswell was the beginning of a government cover-up about UFOs.

ROSWELL COVER-UP?

WASHINGTON, D.C, September 8, 1994—The United States Air Force presented a 23-page report that says what *really* happened near Roswell, New Mexico. In the report, the Air Force said that, yes, an unidentified object did fall to earth 47 years ago- but it was neither a spacecraft nor a weather balloon. It was a very *special* balloon used in a top-secret mission to spy on the Soviet Union. The report added that there were no alien or human bodies found at the crash area.

So, what exactly did those townspeople see back in 1947?

As the story goes, Mac Brazel, a local rancher had been walking in a grassland area when he came upon some trash: a few twisted rubber strips, some paper, sticks and pieces of tin foil. A couple of weeks later, Brazel showed a piece of his discovered material to Loretta Proctor and her husband Floyd (dead since 1985). Loretta remembers how she, her husband, and Mac Brazel took the material and tried to burn it, cut it, and scrape at it, but were unsuccessful in all their tries. Loretta Proctor is now the only one of the three still living.

It seems that there were many reports of UFO sightings in 1947, especially in the western parts of the United States. At that time, Loretta, Floyd, and Mac heard there was a $10,000 reward for anyone who found a UFO. So, Mac took his discovery to the officials at the air base.

The materials reached Major Jesse Marcel, the intelligence officer at Roswell Army Air Field. After looking closely at the materials, Marcel said he believed they were the remains of a UFO crash. Later that day, Mac Brazel's materials were taken away, and according to Loretta Proctor, that was the last time they saw what they had brought. As a matter of fact, says Loretta, that was the last time any of them were ever asked anything about what happened near Roswell. Others who had come to the desert area to see aliens and the spacecraft were never interviewed.

"The Roswell Incident," as it has come to be known, was forgotten for nearly 30 years until 1978. Jesse Marcel, by then a civilian, was interviewed by a tabloid newspaper. He told what Loretta Proctor also says happened- that a UFO crashed in a desert area near Roswell. Many other stories soon arose from former military officials who also say that what was found at Roswell was a UFO and an alien body.

AREA 51

There has been much talk about a secret United States Air Force base in Rachel, Nevada known as Area 51. The base is located 90 miles north of Las Vegas. Area 51 does not need to follow any environmental regulations and its budget is completely secret. Nothing is publicly known about what happens there, but the base has been a test site for many top-secret CIA projects. Some say it is a center for studies on UFOs. According to some investigators who have only seen the base from the outside (and who are chased away by the military as soon as they are noticed) there are some hangars. One hanger is quite big. There is also a control tower. According to their reports, a group of unmarked airliners takes more than 1,500 workers from Las Vegas to the base every work day.

In 1989, Bob Lazar, a former employee of Area 51, told reporters that he saw and worked with alien spacecraft there.

Many UFO researchers believe it is possible that remains of aliens and alien spacecraft, such as what was taken away at Roswell, are being kept there.

HELPFUL VOCABULARY

UFO – unidentified flying object, usually meaning not from Earth
injured – hurt
alien – a creature from another world
military – the armed forces, such as the army and navy
wreckage – the broken parts of something destroyed in an accident
statement – opinion or piece of information given publicly
cover-up – an attempt to prevent people from knowing
spacecraft – spaceship
spy – secretly collect information or watch people usually for a government or a company
local – relating to a special town or area where people live
twisted – turned out of shape
strip – a long, narrow piece of material
scrape – rub something from a surface, using the edge of a knife, stick etc.
authorities – people or organizations in charge of a place
intelligence officer – official who collects information
remains – parts left after something has been destroyed (wreckage)
incident – a happening
civilian – anyone who is not a member of the military or police
tabloid – a newspaper with not much serious news
former – having had a particular position before, but not now
environmental – relating to or affecting air, land or water
regulations – rules or orders
budget – a plan of how to spend available money
public – in a way that is meant for anyone to know, see or hear
investigator – one who tries to find out the truth
chase – quickly follow someone/something to catch him/her/it
hangar – a very large building where aircraft are kept
control tower – a tall structure used for signaling or controlling

RAPID REPLY

Write answers to these questions immediately.

1. When did the UFO land in Roswell?
   a. in the early forties   c. in the late forties
   b. in the mid-forties   d. 40 years ago

2. What did the military do after announcing that an unidentified flying object had landed? _____.

3. (**T-F**) The military said that what landed at Roswell was a weather balloon, not a spaceship.

4. The 1994 report presented by the Air Force explained that the balloon that crashed at Roswell had been used for _____

_____.

5. What did Mac Brazel and Loretta and Floyd Proctor try to do to the material found at the crash site? _____.

6. Who is Loretta Proctor?
    a. a military employee   c. Mac's cousin
    b. a witness, dead since 1985   d. a townsperson

7. How much money could a person get in 1947 for finding a UFO?

8. What do we know about Major Jesse Marcel?
    a. He knew secret government information.
    b. He didn't believe a UFO had crashed in Roswell.
    c. He has no interest in talking about UFOs.
    d. He still works for the military.

9. (**T-F**) Area 51 is open to the public.

A CLOSER LOOK

1. Look at the title of the story. What do you think it means?

    _____

2. List the six most important details of the story here.

    a.

    b.

    c.

    d.

    e.

    f.

    Do you and your classmates agree?

3. Imagine that you are the reporter who wrote this newspaper article. Write a headline that you think would attract readers to your story.

    _____

CLASS EXERCISES

- In small groups, discuss whether you agree or disagree with these statements. Remember to give reasons for your opinions.

1. There is life on other planets.

2. We have been visited by aliens from other planets.

3. I believe the crash at Roswell really happened.

4. The government is covering up the truth that UFOs exist.

5. I would be afraid if the government said that UFOs exist.

6. Space aliens are more advanced than we are.

7. I have seen a UFO.

Co-operActivity

TRUE OR FALSE STORIES

Work with a partner to think of an "incredible" true or false story. Then, tell the story to the class making sure each of you has a part. Be sure to use gestures to make it very exciting. The class must guess if your story is true or false.

CHAPTER 13

To Treat or Not to Treat

WARM-UP

Look at the illustration of each AIDS victim above. In pairs or in a group, discuss the answers to these questions.

1. What do you think happened to these people?

2. What do you think their life was like before they reached their present situation?

3. What do you think their life is like now?

Co-operActivity

THE MISSING WORDS

Read the paragraph below. Work with a partner to fill in each of the blanks with one of the words from the following list.

talk	can	yes	decide	scientists	day	cure

Every _____ AIDS patients hope that _____ will be one step closer to finding a _____ for the disease. Now there is _____ that the new AIDS medicines _____ stop the virus that causes the disease from advancing. But can doctors _____ who will get the new drugs? Apparently, _____! Here's why.

Co-operActivity

PARAGRAPH OUTLINE.

Your teacher will assign you another paragraph of the story. Work together with a group to discuss the contents of the paragraph. Decide if you have a "To Treat" or a "Not to Treat" paragraph. Then, in the form of an outline, write down the main idea of your paragraph, and list the details that support the main idea. When you have finished, find a partner with a different paragraph. Each of you will use your outline to explain the contents of your paragraph.

Example: I. Main Idea
         A. Supporting detail
         B. Supporting detail
           1. Smaller detail
             a. Detail
             b. Detail
           2. Smaller detail
         C. Supporting detail
           1. Smaller detail
           2. Smaller detail

TO TREAT OR NOT TO TREAT

AIDS and ETHICS

Of all diseases caused by viruses, AIDS is considered the most serious and difficult to cure. A virus makes a person sick by entering cells in the body. Then, it uses material in those cells, multiplying until it kills the cell. A virus could even kill the organ of which the cell is a part, and perhaps even the whole body itself.

Normally, when a virus enters a body, attack cells discover it, devour it and protect the body to keep it healthy. But, when the Human Immunodeficiency Virus (HIV), the virus known to cause AIDS, enters the body, it kills the attack cells, and so leaves a person with no fighting power against other diseases.

Every day AIDS patients hope that scientists will be one step closer to finding a cure for the disease. Now there is talk that the new AIDS medicines can stop the virus that causes the disease from advancing. But can doctors decide who will get the new drugs? Apparently, yes! Here's why.

According to a report in *The New York Times*, doctors are not giving the new drugs to "unreliable" patients, specifically the homeless and drug addicts. Doctors say have made their decisions using scientific fact.

The H.I.V. virus is known to multiply and mutate quickly. If AIDS patients do not take the new medicine regularly, the virus will become drug-resistant. And if the drug-resistant virus spreads, the new medicines presently being used will not work and that would cause even more health problems for people.

"But it is dangerous to refuse anyone new drugs," says Daniel Baxter, assistant director of Casa Promesa, an AIDS treatment center in New York. He wrote an article that appeared in *The New York Times*. As he explains it, when the news is heard that these newer drugs are successful, more AIDS victims will want them. "The fact that some people will not be given treatment," Baxter tells us, "will probably cause black-market sales of the medicines." So, if there are AIDS and H.I.V. victims who know they will not be able to get the newer medicines through a doctor, they will try to get them through the black market, and then, give themselves the medicine with no medical supervision.

"Without giving these "unreliable" people a chance, how do we know who will or won't be a good candidate for the new medicine?" asks Baxter in his article.

HELPFUL VOCABULARY

AIDS – Anti Immune Deficiency Syndrome

HIV – Human Immunodeficiency Virus

virus – a tiny non-living thing which when absorbed by a living cell can make many copies of itself, eventually destroying the cell, the organ and even the body of which it is a part

cell – the smallest unit of any living thing which can reproduce (make a copy of) itself

organ – part of the body, e.g. heart, lung, kidney,

devour – eat up

unreliable – not dependable

mutate – to change in form, quality or nature

drug-resistant – not affected by a drug

spread – to get bigger or worse

refuse – say no to

victim – one who is affected by a bad situation

treatment – a method intended to cure a sickness or injury

black-market – the system by which people illegally buy and sell goods, etc. that are difficult to get

candidate – a person who applies for a job or a position

RAPID REPLY

Answer these questions immediately.

1. This story is mainly about
   a. people with AIDS.
   b. black-market sales of medicines.
   c. who gets AIDS treatment.
   d. new AIDS medications.

2. According to the article, which people are considered "unreliable?"

   _____.

3. (**T-F**) As the H.I.V virus multiplies it also changes its form.

4. (**T-F**) If someone with AIDS doesn't take the drugs regularly, the drugs soon won't be effective in attacking the virus.

5. Who is Daniel Baxter? _____.

6. A black market is
   a. an illegal system for buying and selling things.
   b. a food store that stays open after 11:00 p.m.
   c. an area where evening events such as parties or lectures take place.

7. Why does Daniel Baxter see the possible development of a black market to get the newer AIDS medicines?

   _____.

8. Is Baxter for or against giving unreliable AIDS victims the newer

   medicines? _____.

A CLOSER LOOK

1. Look at the title of the story. What do you think it means?

   _____

2. Imagine that you are the reporter who wrote this newspaper article. Write a headline that you think would attract readers to your story.

   _____

CLASS EXERCISES

- In small groups, discuss your opinions about these questions.
   1. What do you know about AIDS?
   2. Do you know anyone who has AIDS?
   3. Would you send your child to school if you knew a student there had AIDS?
   4. Do you think it was a good idea that Magic Johnson retired from professional basketball because he has the H.I.V. virus?
   5. Should doctors give the new AIDS medicine to "unreliable" people with AIDS?

QUICK-WRITE

A quick-write is a chance to write without stopping to make corrections.

You are an "unreliable" AIDS patient. Write a letter to a doctor explaining why you need a chance to join the program for the new AIDS treatment.

Date: _____

Dear Doctor,

_____

_____

_____

_____

_____

_____

_____

_____

_____

_____

_____

_____

_____

Sincerely,

_____

Co-operActivity

FACTS AND OPINIONS EXCHANGE

Work with your group or partner to write four questions – two factual, two opinion, based on the information presented in the article. Write the questions on an index card or a sheet of paper. When you have finished, exchange your index cards with another group, and discuss the answers to the questions your classmates made.

CHAPTER 14
Standing Tall

WARM-UP *Co-operActivity: COMPARING GUESSES*

Work with a partner to fill in the missing word(s) of the story you are about to read. Be sure to use contextual clues to help you fill in the blanks. Compare your guesses with other students. Support your choices.

Bruce Anderson works as a _____. Early Tuesday morning before

he started to work, his supervisor gave him a bunch of _____

to give out to his passengers to try to encourage more people to _____

_____. Bruce told his supervisor that he would not pass out _____

_____ because he didn't believe in _____

_____. Bruce's supervisor fired him for refusing to do his job.

Co-operActivity: YOU'RE HOT / YOU'RE COLD

You have a chance to get the actual details of the story by playing the *You're hot, You're cold* guessing game with your teacher. S/he will tell you if your guesses are "getting warmer" (closer) to the actual details of the story.

STANDING TALL

Defending your beliefs

ORANGE COUNTY, California, June 6, 1996—Bruce Anderson is a bus driver. One Tuesday morning Bruce got up, got dressed and went to work not knowing that by the end of the day his name, his job and his lifestyle would become national news. Here's what happened.

Bruce Anderson, 38, has been a bus driver for Orange County for five years. Early Tuesday morning as he was about to leave the bus station to start his route, a supervisor gave him a stack of coupons to pass out to his passengers. Each coupon was worth a free hamburger from a well-known hamburger restaurant chain. The coupons, Anderson was told, were being used to encourage people to take the bus by offering them free hamburgers each Tuesday for the month of June.

Bruce told the supervisor that he would not give out the coupons to his passengers because of his belief that killing and eating animals is wrong. Bruce Anderson is a strict vegetarian. He does not eat meat or dairy products or wear things made of leather. He told the supervisor that he did not want to support the fast-food restaurant in their slaughtering of cows. Then, he left to begin his route.

Approximately half an hour later, transportation officials met him at a bus stop with a replacement driver, ordered him off the bus in front of his passengers, and later, fired him for refusing to do his job.

According to an official of the transportation company who was interviewed by reporters, "Passing out coupons is part of a bus driver's job, like handing out transfers or calling out stops. He is a bus driver for the city—a job that has lot of responsibility. He was not following orders."

Anderson was embarrassed by the way he was told to get off his bus during his work schedule. He told reporters, "I'm paid to drive a bus, not sit there and hand out coupons for something I don't believe in."

Anderson has support from the local animal rights group he belongs to. Stating her view about Anderson's situation, Ava Park, founder of Orange County People for Animals told reporters, "It's a First Amendment issue. You don't leave your ethics at the door when you go to work. He is being asked to pass out advertisements opposed to his ethical beliefs. This is a case of bullying."

HELPUL VOCABULARY

stack – an neat pile

encourage – make something more likely to happen

strict – rule-obeying; inflexible

dairy – milk and milk products

slaughter – to kill

route – the pathway from one place to another

official – one who has a responsible position in an organization

replacement – substitute

oppose – disagree strongly with an idea or action

ethical – relating to what is right or wrong

bullying – threatening to hurt or frighten someone weaker or smaller

file a lawsuit – bring a problem or complaint to court to be settled, especially for money

suffer – experience painful effects

compensation – money paid to someone for injury, loss, or damage

RAPID REPLY

Write answers to these questions immediately.

1. When and where did this story take place? _____.

2. What is Bruce Anderson's job? _____.

3. Which statement is **not** grammatically correct?

   As Bruce was about to leave the bus station,

       a. his supervisor gives him a stack of coupons.

       b. he was given a stack of coupons by his supervisor.

       c. his supervisor gave him a stack of coupons.

4. (**T-F**) With these coupons, passengers could ride the bus free each Tuesday for the month of June.

5. Why didn't Bruce want to give out the coupons to his passengers?

   _____.

6. We know that Anderson felt embarrassed when he was replaced by another bus driver because

       a. he got off the bus without saying how he felt.

       b. the bus officials replaced him without warning him first.

       c. the passengers on the bus saw everything.

7. (**T-F**) The transportation company official said that Bruce was fired because he was not following orders.

8. Which organization has given Bruce their support and why?

   _____.

9. What is Bruce Anderson really fighting for?

       a. the freedom to follow his beliefs

       b. the right to receive his lost earnings

       c. the ability to change his bad situation

Co-operActivity

RETELL THE STORY

Sit in a circle. The class is going to retell the story in sequence, sentence by sentence. The first person begins with, "This story is about..." Then, moving clockwise, the next person continues the story, adding another sentence. Follow along the circle so that each person has at least one turn to add a sentence to complete the story. If you get stuck and can't remember what comes next, ask your teacher for a key word to jog your memory.

More Information

- Some reports said that Anderson did offer to take the coupons on that Tuesday and leave them stacked at the front of the bus for passengers to see and take for themselves.

- Anderson offered to take another bus-related job in the company until the burger coupon-program was finished.

- Bruce Anderson is filing a lawsuit saying that the Orange County Transportation Authority is discriminating against him because of his ethical beliefs. Anderson wants his job back and is also asking for monetary compensation for his mental pain and emotional suffering. He is also seeking compensation for his lost earnings.

A CLOSER LOOK

1. Look at the title of the story. What do you think it means?

   _____

2. List the four most important details of the story here.

   a.

   b.

   c.

   d.

   Do you and your classmates agree?

3. Imagine that you are the reporter who wrote this newspaper article. Write a headline that you think would attract readers to your story.

   _____

Co-operActivity

WORD ASSOCIATIONS

In pairs or in a group, discuss how you think each of these words relates to the word "freedom." Give examples for your opinions wherever possible.

encourage	suffer	oppose	beliefs
government	lifestyle	responsibility	

CLASS EXERCISES

- In small groups, discuss your opinions about the questions below.

  1. Should Bruce Anderson have been fired from his job?

     Together as a group, list the reasons why someone might think Bruce should have been fired.

     a.

     b.

     c.

     d.

     Together as a group, list the reasons why someone might think Bruce shouldn't have been fired.

     a.

     b.

     c.

     d.

Write **your** opinion here.

_____

_____

_____

_____.

2. With your group, discuss why you would or wouldn't become a vegetarian.

3. Tell your group about a time when you had to fight for something you believed in.

Co-operActivity

CLASSROOM FEUD

Your teacher will use some words from the story. You and your team will have the chance to test your ability to use new vocabulary correctly in a sentence. The object of the game is to score as many points for your team as possible. Raise your flag or sound your noisemaker to signal that you are ready to say your sentence. Remember, your sentence must make sense and be grammatically correct to receive a point. If it isn't, the other team will have a chance to score the point. The first team to score 10 points is the winner. GOOD LUCK!

Co-operActivity

DIALOG ROLE-PLAY

In pairs or in a group, choose one paragraph of the story, write a dialog, and act it out in front of the class.

CHAPTER 15

Given Half a Chance

WARM-UP

In pairs or in a group, discuss your ideas about the following situation.

Imagine that your friend is the owner of a small grocery store. It has taken him many years to build this successful business. He and his family live on the earnings of this store. Business has been very good, but the store has been robbed five times in the past two years. Your friend is thinking about buying a gun to protect himself and the store from future robberies.

1. What advice would you give your friend?
2. Do you think everyone has the right to own a gun for self-protection?
3. Would you consider owning a gun?
4. Is there much crime activity in your neighborhood?

Co-operActivity

TIMED READING

You will read the story of Yoshihiro Hattori paragraph by paragraph with a partner. You and your partner may answer the timed-reading questions that follow to help you better understand the people and events in the story.

When you have finished the story, you are going to take part in a police line-up either as one of the characters in the story or as part of the audience. If you are chosen to be one of the characters in the story, don't be too shy to defend yourself! If you are a member of the audience, try to get specific answers to your questions from the characters.

For the last activity of this chapter, you are going to participate in an actual trial, so that you can become familiar with the American court justice system. You will play one of the characters in the story, be a member of the jury, or represent a member of the audience. When you have chosen your role in the trial, refer to your trial-preparation assignment in the chapter.

GIVEN HALF A CHANCE

Gun control in America

BATON ROUGE, Louisiana, October 17, 1992—What exactly was Rodney Peairs thinking when those two young teenagers came up the driveway of his home that cool autumn evening? Here is the story of how a misunderstanding and a gun ended someone's life.

Yoshihiro Hattori, a 16 year-old student from Japan, had come to the United States on an exchange program. He was living with the Haymaker family at their home in Baton Rouge and was attending the local high school with the Haymaker's son, Webb.

On the evening of October 17, 1992, Yoshihiro and Webb were looking for a Halloween party to which they had been invited. Not knowing the area very well, the boys parked the car in the drive-way of the house where they thought the party was being held. They parked behind a pick-up truck.

Since this was to be a costume party, both boys were dressed up. Webb was dressed as someone who had been in an accident with his arm in a splint and a bandage around his head. He wore no makeup and there was no blood on his costume. Since Yoshihiro loved to dance, he came dressed as a John Travolta disco character with a white jacket, black pants and a white ruffled shirt unbuttoned to the middle of his chest. Yoshihiro was also carrying a camera.

Not knowing they had parked at the wrong house, Webb and Yoshihiro walked up the driveway and rang the front doorbell. They heard the noise of window blinds moving at the window to their left and walked towards the window. They saw a small boy, perhaps eight or nine years old, looking through the blinds. Suddenly, the front door opened and a woman wearing a bathrobe and glasses appeared. Webb began to speak as both boys walked towards her, but before Webb could say anything, she slammed the door.

At that point, the boys walked back down the driveway toward their parked car. Webb was now pretty sure that they were at the wrong house and tried to explain the situation to Yoshihiro. As he looked back at the house, Webb saw a man standing in the doorway with a large handgun. Yoshihiro, who was not wearing his contact lenses, turned towards the man and shouted, "We're here for the party!"

Yoshihiro started walking back up the driveway towards the house. Webb, called his friend back, but Yoshihiro continued to walk towards the man explaining

(Continued on the next page)

Given Half a Chance

(Continued from previous page)

that they had come to this house looking for a party. As Yoshihiro got closer, the man yelled, "Freeze!" The young Japanese student had no idea that he had just been given a signal to stop and walked a little closer towards the man. It was there that the man in the doorway shot Yoshihiro in the chest. Yoshihiro fell to the ground on his back. Webb immediately got the next-door neighbors to call for an ambulance, and on the way to the hospital, Yoshihiro died.

Rodney Peairs went to trial for manslaughter, a crime for which he could go to jail for up to 11 years.

At the trial, Rodney and Bonnie Peairs told the court that when they heard the doorbell that night they sent their stepson to the window to see who it was. Mrs. Peairs decided to answer the door, but when she saw a person in bandages and an Asian man coming towards her, she became frightened and quickly shut the door. She yelled to her husband, Rodney, "Get the gun!"

Rodney Peairs told the court that he had never seen his wife so frightened. He ran to the bedroom, followed by his wife and three children and got his .44 magnum revolver from the top shelf of the closet. Then, he ran to the front door, opened it, and stood there looking past his pickup truck at Webb and Yoshihiro who were standing at the end of his driveway. Bonnie was standing next to him on the right. With the poor lighting at the front door, Rodney explained, he was able to see that a 5'7" Asian man was coming toward him. The man seemed to be laughing and carrying something in his left hand. Raising his gun with both hands, Rodney shouted for the man to "Freeze;" but the stranger continued walking toward him, talking about something Rodney was unable to understand. It was then that Rodney fired his gun, hitting Yoshihiro in the chest. Rodney ran back into the house, shut the door, and told his wife to call 911. The Peairs family closed all the windows and waited together in the kitchen for the police to arrive.

HELPFUL VOCABULARY

local – relating to a particular place or area

costume – clothes worn to make you look like someone/something

splint – flat piece of wood or metal attached to a person's body to keep a broken bone from moving

bandage – piece of cloth wrapped around an injured part of the body

ruffle – a band of cloth sewn in folds to decorate clothing

blinds – cloth or other material that you pull down to cover a window

slammed – close with a lot of force

contact lenses – small, round piece of plastic or glass worn in the eye to help you see more clearly

bullet – small, round piece of metal shot from a gun

ambulance – special car for taking sick/injured people to the hospital

go to trial – take part in a legal process in which a court of law examines a case to decide whether a person is guilty of a crime

manslaughter – the crime of killing someone without intending to

frightened – scared; afraid

• Timed-Reading Questions

Paragraph 1

— Which three people does this paragraph introduce?

— What events does this paragraph tell about?

Paragraph 2

— How old was Yoshihiro Hattori?

— Why was he in the United States?

— Who is Webb?

Paragraph 3

— Where were the boys going that evening?

— How did the boys get there?

— Did they find the right house?

Paragraph 4

— How was Webb dressed?

— How was Yoshihiro dressed?

— Why was Yoshihiro dressed that way?

Paragraph 5

— Did the boys know they had come to the wrong house?

— Who was at the window?

— Did the woman at the door talk to the two young men?

— How do you know she was not expecting visitors?

— Why did she slam the door?

Paragraph 6

— What did Webb finally realize?

— Why do you think Yoshihiro didn't notice that the man at the doorway was carrying a gun?

Paragraph 7

— What did Yoshihiro want to explain to the man at the door?

— Why did the man holding the gun yell, "Freeze!"?

— How do you know Yoshihiro didn't understand that word?

— What happened to Yoshihiro?

Paragraph 8

— For what crime might Rodney Peairs go to jail?

— What is the most time Rodney Peairs could spend in jail?

Paragraph 9

— What did the Peairs do when they heard the doorbell?

— According to Mrs. Peairs, why did she slam the door?

— What did Mrs. Peairs do after she slammed the door?

Paragraph 10

— Why did Rodney get the gun?

— Where was the gun?

— What makes you think that perhaps Rodney could not see the boys so clearly?

— What did Rodney do after he shot Yoshihiro?

A CLOSER LOOK

1. Look at the title of the story. What do you think it means?

   _____

2. List the four most important details of the story here.

   a.

   b.

   c.

   d.

   Do you and your classmates agree?

3. Below are 11 individual statements. Some are facts; some are opinions. Label each statement using **F** for **FACT** and **O** for **OPINION** in the space provided.

   ___ Yoshihiro Hattori was an exchange student in the United States.

   ___ He really enjoyed living in his "new" country.

   ___ Yoshihiro was pleased to be dressed as the John Travolta disco character.

   ___ Yoshihiro was carrying a camera that evening.

   ___ The boys parked in the driveway of Rodney Peairs' house.

   ___ A small boy was looking through the window.

   ___ Yoshihiro could not see that Rodney Peairs had a handgun because he was not wearing his contact lenses.

   ___ Yoshihiro said, "We're here for the party."

   ___ Rodney Peairs shot Yoshihiro because he was afraid for his family's safety.

   ___ Mrs. Peairs had never been so frightened as she was that evening when she saw the two boys.

   ___ The Peairs family waited in the kitchen for the police to arrive.

Co-operActivity

THE POLICE LINE-UP

You will see the names of the major characters on the board—Yoshihiro Hattori, Webb Haymaker, Rodney Peairs, Mrs. Peairs, the stepson, the next-door neighbors, Mr. and Mrs. Haymaker, Mr. and Mrs. Hattori.

In police line-up style, your teacher will select one student at a time to stand at the board under a character name while the rest of the students shout out any questions or comments they have about that character and his or her part in the story. This exercise should help you to review the events of the story.

Co-operActivity

THE TRIAL

Look on the following pages for your trial-preparation assignment. You must take this activity seriously to make the trial as authentic as possible. Prepare your assignment thoroughly, looking at all opportunities you have to affect the outcome of the trial.

Read the information about the American court justice system and the arguments for and against "The right to bear arms" (right to own guns) before you begin to prepare for the trial.

The American criminal justice system is based on the idea that allowing a guilty person to go free is better than putting an innocent person in jail. That is why the prosecution (in this case, the Hattori family's lawyer) has an extra difficult job. Rodney Peairs is considered innocent of manslaughter until the prosecution can prove beyond a reasonable doubt that he is guilty.

The Second Amendment to the Constitution says that "A well—regulated militia, being necessary to the security of a free State, the right of the people to keep and bear arms, shall not be infringed." To date, this has meant that it is legal for people in the United States to own guns.

BASIC ARGUMENT FOR A PERSON'S RIGHT TO BEAR ARMS

Some people believe that the Second Amendment, which is part of the Bill of Rights—laws that were written to protect *individual* freedoms against unfair rule by the national government, was meant to give people the right to protect themselves, their family and their friends if they are in danger.

BASIC ARGUMENT AGAINST A PERSON'S RIGHT TO BEAR ARMS

Some people believe that the Second Amendment is not an *individual* right. It doesn't mean that individual people have the right to own guns. These people believe that the word "militia" in the amendment refers to "the military." Others say that the amendment was written to limit the power of the national government and give more power to the state governments, not to individual people. In this way, the state could protect the people of the United States and keep order by using a police force. So, the words "the right of the people to bear arms" refers to the right of a police force to have guns, not individual citizens.

TRIAL ROLE ASSIGNMENTS

WEBB HAYMAKER

ROLE: You are a key witness for the prosecution. You must give the facts of that evening when Yoshihiro was shot. You should wear a suit or a pair of nice pants and a buttoned-down shirt to the trial.

FOCUS: You want Rodney Peairs to go to jail for killing your friend. You believe Rodney Peairs shot his gun in order to kill Yoshihiro. In other words, you believe that it was his plan to kill Yoshihiro with his gun, rather than just scare or hurt him. You believe that you and Yoshihiro presented no danger to Rodney Peairs.

QUESTIONS: The prosecution lawyer will ask you the following questions to which you must give clear answers. Work together with the "audience", your classmates who are for the prosecution, to help you prepare the answers for the trial.

1. Tell the court your name and what you do.
2. Describe your relationship with Yoshihiro Hattori.
3. Why did you go to Rodney Peairs' house?
4. Describe your costume.
5. Did you try to speak to Mrs. Peairs when she answered the door?
6. What did you want to tell her?
7. Why didn't Yoshihiro stop when Rodney Peairs yelled, "Freeze!"
8. What did you do after Yoshihiro was shot?

Be prepared! The defense lawyer (Rodney Peairs' lawyer) is going to ask you some questions about that evening.

TRIAL ROLE ASSIGNMENTS

PROSECUTION LAWYER

ROLE: You are the prosecution lawyer, representing the people of the State of Louisiana. You believe that Yoshihiro and Webb presented no danger to Rodney Peairs to make him shoot his gun. You should be dressed nicely to present your case.

FOCUS:: Start with an opening statement to the jury. Tell them that you plan to prove that Yoshihiro Hattori did not, in any way, present a danger to Rodney Peairs or his family. Tell the jury that studies have shown that about 15 children die every day from gunshots, and accidents involving guns are now the number one cause of death for teenage boys. Next, tell the events of the story in order of how they happened. In your closing statement, tell the jury that people who own guns, like Rodney Peairs, should be educated in gun safety and should realize how powerful and how dangerous guns are.

QUESTIONS: Ask Webb the following questions.

1. Tell the court your name and what you do.
2. Describe your relationship with Yoshihiro Hattori.
3. Why did you go to Rodney Peairs' house?
4. Describe your costume.
5. Did you try to speak to Mrs. Peairs when she answered the door?
6. What did you want to tell her?
7. Why didn't Yoshihiro stop when Rodney Peairs yelled, "Freeze!"
8. What did you do after Yoshihiro was shot?

With the help of your classmates on Yoshihiro's side, make up to 4 questions each to ask Rodney Peairs, Bonnie Peairs (Rodney's wife), and the stepson.

TRIAL ROLE ASSIGNMENTS

RODNEY PEAIRS

ROLE: You are a defendant. You must give the facts of that evening when you shot Yoshihiro. You should wear a suit or a pair of nice pants and a buttoned-down shirt to the trial.

FOCUS: You do not want to go to jail for manslaughter. You believe you shot Yoshihiro in self-defense. You believe that Yoshihiro presented a danger to you and your family that night.

QUESTIONS: The defense lawyer (your lawyer) will ask you the following questions to which you must give clear answers. Work together with the "audience" – your classmates who are for the defense – to help you prepare the answers for the trial.

1. Tell the court your name.
2. What kind of neighborhood do you live in?
3. Were you expecting any visitors on the evening of October 17, 1992?
4. How were the two strangers dressed?
5. Why did you get your gun?
6. Describe the lighting at your front door?
7. Was Webb Haymaker's car the only car in the driveway?
8. Did you try to warn Yoshihiro that you had a gun?
9. Could you see Yoshihiro clearly when you shot him?
10. What did you do after you shot Yoshihiro?

Be prepared! The prosecution lawyer is going to ask you some questions about that evening.

TRIAL ROLE ASSIGNMENTS

DEFENSE LAWYER

ROLE: You are the defense lawyer, the lawyer for Rodney Peairs. You believe that Yoshihiro and Webb presented a danger to Rodney Peairs and his family to make him shoot his gun. You should dress nicely to present your case.

FOCUS: Start with an opening statement to the jury. Tell them that you plan to prove that Rodney Peairs acted in self-defense when he shot Yoshihiro to protect himself and his family from danger. Tell the jury that the Second Amendment gives every American the right to carry a gun for protection against danger. Next, tell the events of the story in order of how they happened. In your closing statement, tell the jury that Rodney Peairs was trying to protect himself and his family from a stranger who did not belong near his home. Say, again, that the lighting at the front door was poor and that Rodney tried to warn Yoshihiro that he had a gun.

QUESTIONS: Ask Rodney the following questions.

1. Tell the court your name.
2. What kind of neighborhood do you live in?
3. Were you expecting any visitors on the evening of October 17, 1992?
4. How were the two strangers dressed?
5. Why did you get your gun?
6. Describe the lighting at your front door?
7. Was Webb Haymaker's car the only car in the driveway?
8. Did you try to warn Yoshihiro that you had a gun?
9. Could you see Yoshihiro clearly when you shot him?
10. What did you do after you shot Yoshihiro?

With the help of your classmates on Rodney's side, make up to 4 questions each to ask Webb Haymaker, Bonnie Peairs (Rodney's wife), and the stepson.

TRIAL ROLE ASSIGNMENTS

BONNIE PEAIRS

ROLE: You are a key witness for the defense. You must give the facts of that evening when your husband shot Yoshihiro. You should wear a suit, a dress, or a pair of nice pants and blouse to the trial.

FOCUS: You do not want your husband to go to jail for manslaughter. You believe he shot Yoshihiro in self-defense. You were not expecting any visitors on the evening of October 17, 1992. You were so frightened by the two strangers at the front door — especially the stranger in bandages, that you told your husband to get the gun. You believe that Yoshihiro presented a danger to you and your family that night.

QUESTIONS: The defense lawyer (your husband's lawyer) and the prosecution lawyer will ask you questions to which you must give clear answers.

THE STEPSON

ROLE: You are a key witness for the defense. You are eight or nine years old. You must tell about what happened on the evening of October 17, 1992. You should wear nice, clean clothes to the trial.

FOCUS: You do not want your father to go to jail. When your parents sent you to the window after the doorbell rang, you saw two strangers through the window blinds.

QUESTIONS: The defense lawyer (your father's lawyer) and the prosecution lawyer will ask you questions to which you must give clear answers.

THE BAILIFF

ROLE: Your job is to call the court to order and swear in the witnesses. (See the information below.) You should wear some kind of police-looking uniform to the trial. You will stand or sit on the side of the courtroom near the judge. Be sure not to block anybody's view.

FOCUS: Try to memorize your lines. When the judge enters the courtroom you must say the following to everyone in the courtroom:

"All rise." (Be sure that everyone stands up.) "The honorable Judge _____ (say your teacher's name) presiding. The court is now in session. Please be seated and come to order."

When a witness is called, you must swear the witness in before s/he sits in the witness chair. Say the following:

"Raise your right hand. Do you solemnly affirm that the testimony you give this court shall be the truth, the whole truth, and nothing but the truth."

Be sure that the witness answers, "I do." before s/he takes a seat in the witness chair.

AUDIENCE FOR THE PROSECUTION

ROLE: You are a member of the audience on the side of the prosecution. You believe that Rodney Peairs should go to jail for manslaughter for the death of Yoshihiro. You believe that handguns are bad and cause too many unnecessary deaths in this country. You believe there should be more laws regulating who can own a gun in America. Background checks and waiting periods for people who want to buy guns has been a good change, but you think more needs to be done. For example, owners should be educated in gun safety and be required to pass a test to get a gun license. Gun owners should pay some kind of annual tax for owning a gun and have insurance in case of a gun-related accident.

ASSIGNMENT:

1. Help the prosecution lawyer make up questions to ask Rodney Peairs, Bonnie Peairs, and the stepson that will convince the jury to put Rodney in jail for unnecessarily killing Yoshihiro Hattori.

2. Help Webb Haymaker prepare his answers to his assigned questions for the trial.

3. Make a sign to show that you are for more government control of guns.

4. Bring your sign on the day of the trial.

5. Before the trial begins, shout out your opinions about gun control.

TRIAL ROLE ASSIGNMENTS

AUDIENCE FOR THE DEFENSE

ROLE: You are a member of the audience on the side of the defense. You believe that Rodney Peairs should not go to jail for manslaughter for the death of Yoshihiro. You believe that owning a handgun is an individual right of the people as written in the United States Constitution. You do not want the government to interfere in your freedom to "bear arms." You believe it is a basic right of an individual to protect his/her home and family from dangerous situations.

ASSIGNMENT:

1. Help the defense lawyer make up questions to ask Webb Haymaker.
2. Help Rodney Peairs prepare his answers to his assigned questions for the trial.
3. Make a sign to show that you are against more government control of guns.
4. Bring your sign on the day of the trial.
5. Before the trial begins, shout out your opinions against gun control.

JUROR

ROLE: You are one of the jury members. You are not allowed to talk to anyone about the case. You should dress nicely for the trial. One juror (the foreperson) will be chosen to read the jury's decision.

FOCUS: Your job is to listen to the statements made by the witnesses and the lawyers and take notes on what you hear. After the lawyers ask their witnesses questions and give their closing statements, you and the other members of the jury will leave the courtroom to discuss what you heard. As a group you must decide whether Rodney Peairs intentionally meant to kill Yoshihiro. If you think he is guilty of manslaughter, you must decide how many years he will spend in jail. Remember, your vote must be unanimous.

ASSIGNMENT: Research the topic of gun control before the day of the trial. Write down three things you learned from your research.

SURVEY PAGE

Subject:_____

Name	Opinion (for/against)	Comments

SURVEY PAGE

Subject:_____

Name	**Opinion** (for/against)	**Comments**

SURVEY PAGE

Subject:_____

Name	Opinion (for/against)	Comments

SURVEY PAGE

Subject:_____

Name	Opinion (for/against)	Comments

SURVEY PAGE

Subject:_____

Name	Opinion (for/against)	Comments

SURVEY PAGE

Subject:_____

Name	**Opinion** (for/against)	**Comments**

SURVEY PAGE

Subject: _____

Name	**Opinion** (for/against)	**Comments**

Sources

If The Shoe Were On The Other Foot...? — "Father Kills Dog That Mauled His Son", Associated Press, *The Fresno Bee,* 8/5/95 and "Man Who Fatally Beat Dog Charged With Cruelty," David Reyes, *Los Angeles Times*, 8/9/95, Orange County Edition

A Test Of Honesty — "Identity Crisis," *People* Magazine, 5/18/92, Microsoft Internet Explorer, *Dalton v. Educational Testing Serv.*, 87 N.Y.2d 384 (12/7/95), Princeton Review at www.tpr.com.tw/champion.htm and "Test Firm Fights to Reject Suspicious Scores," *The Detroit News*, 8/19/95

Up In Smoke — " Teacher Sues After Being Fired For 20-Year-Old Pot Bust," *Times National News*, 4/6/96, "Blind Justice," *People* Magazine, 5/27/96 and www.archive.org...-alcantu-/smokedope.htm

On Guard — "Troubled Waters," *People* Magazine, 4/29/96 and "Deaf Lifeguard Sues YMCA To Regain His Job" by Robin Estrin, Associated Press, 2/4/96

Really, Really Getting Rid Of Smallpox — "Group Advises Destruction of Smallpox Vaccine," from *News For You*, a publication of New Readers Press. 1996, Prodigy Web Browser: http://www.who.ch/press/1994 and1996, and discussions with Jonathan Said, Chief of Anatomical Pathology — UCLA School of Medicine. *Eat Better, Live Better*, Reader's Digest Association Inc., Pleasantville, NY 1987; *The Super Pyramid*, Dr. Gene Spiller, Time Books, Random House Inc. NY 1993

A Pilot's Bill Of Rights — "Thrown For A Loop," *People* Magazine, 9/19/94, and "Statement On Bob Hoover," *FAA News Release*, 10/18/95.

Troubled Waters — "Controversy Over Fate Of Lake Puts Town, State At Odds," *Los Angeles Times*, 3/22/97 and www.greatbasin.net/~unique/ ElectricNevada, 1996

A Long, Long Time Ago... — "Mayor Can't Shelve His Crime And Punishment," by Mike Clary, *Los Angeles Times*, March 1997.

Got A Cigarette? — "First Arguments Due in Key Suit Against Tobacco Company," *Los Angeles Times*, 4/97, the Internet – http://www.cnnfn.com/news9605/ 15/tobacco and http://www.courttv.com/library/business/tobacco/

Is Shakespeare Really Dead? — "Word of Bard's Death Premature: Can Shakespeare Hold His Own Against Science Fiction," *Los Angeles Times*, 3/25/97 and conversations with Max Nieman, Professor of Political Science and Associate Dean of the College of Humanities, Arts and Social Sciences at the University of California at Riverside, and a personal interview with Dr. Herbert Lindenberger, Professor of Humanities in Comparative Literature and English at Stanford University.

Whose Child Is He, Anyway? — "The Ties that Bind," *People* Magazine, 8/15/94 and www.saf.org/ ccrkba. org/pub/rkba/wais/data Supreme Court of the United States, 2/13/95

Do You Believe…? — Netscape on the Internet, http://www.ufomind.com and "A Saucer Scorned" from *People*, 10/31/94

To Treat Or Not To Treat — "Casting Off The 'Unreliable' AIDS Patient," *The New York Times*, 3/6/97 and JAMA – CDC AIDS Daily Summary, 3/6/97

Standing Tall — The Internet, "The On Going Saga of Vegan Bus Driver 'Bruce Anderson'," http://www.newveg.av.org/BusDriver.htm

Given Half A Chance — Louisiana Case Law, *Hattori vs.Peairs*, 95 0144 (La.App. 1 Cir. 10/6/95); 662 So.2d 509, and The University of Tennessee's *The Daily Beacon* http://beacon-www.asa.utk.edu/issues/v73/n60/japan.60n.html

Comics and Conversation

More Comics and Conversation

Foreign Students' Guide to Pronunciation

Begin in English, Volumes 1, 2 and 3

*Motivational Strategies: Text and Transparencies in Composition
and Grammar*

From the Beginning: A First Reader in American History

Rhythm and Role Play: Text

Rhythm and Role Play: Audio Cassette

Decision Dramas

Americana–Historical Spotlights in Story and Song

Americana–"Easy Reader" Historical Spotlights in Story and Song

Americana–Historical Spotlights in Song, Audio Cassette

47% American–Coping with Cultural Issues in Middle School
Teachers Guide including complete Student Text

47% American–Coping with Cultural Issues in Middle School
Student Text

Please write for our latest brochure.